About this workbook

This book contains questions to target every topic in Year 1 Maths.

- Questions split into three levels of increasing difficulty – Challenge 1, Challenge 2 and Challenge 3 – to aid progress.
- 'How am I doing?' checks for self-evaluation.
- Total marks boxes for each topic.
- Starter test recaps early number skills.
- Four progress tests allow children to test how well they have remembered the information.
- QR codes link to online interactive quizzes for extra practice.
- Progress test charts to record results and identify which areas need further practice.

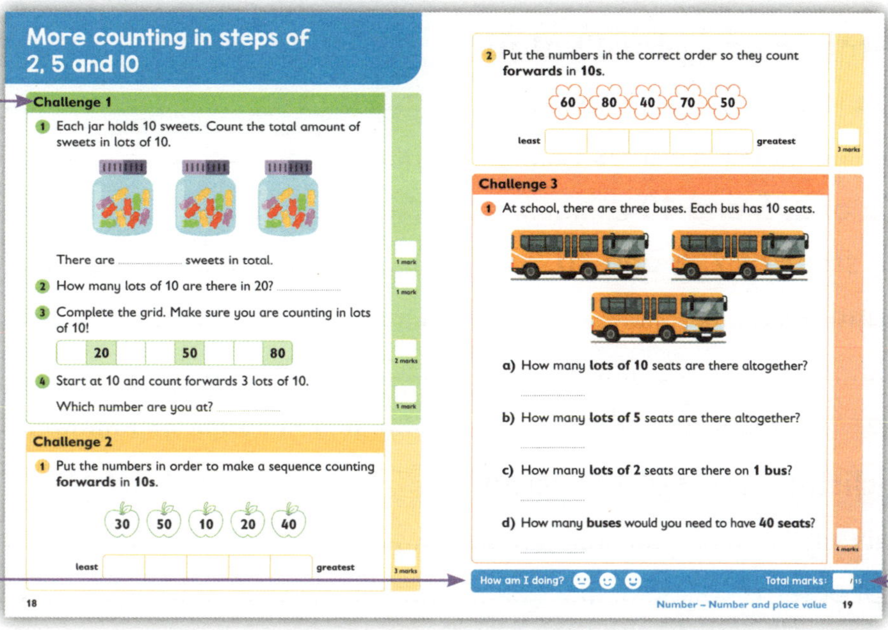

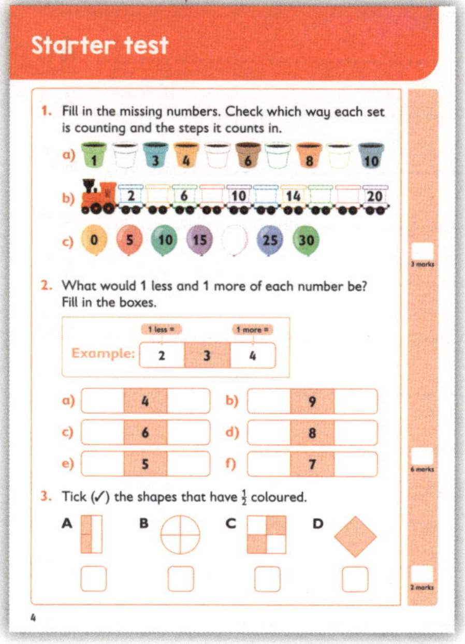

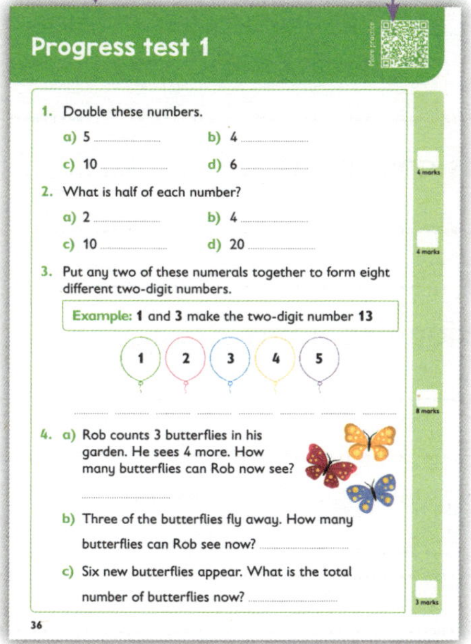

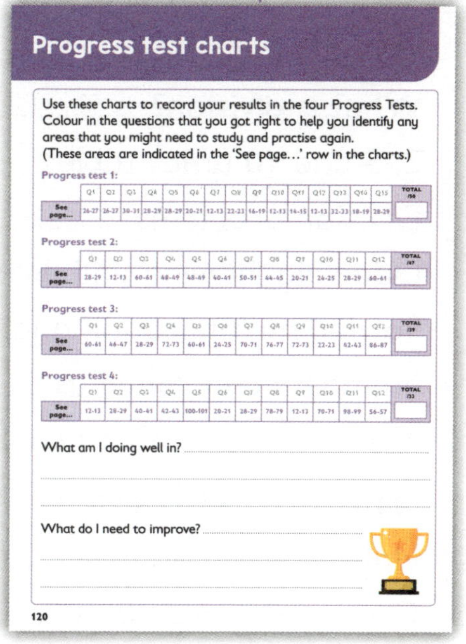

Answers are included at the back of the book.

Author: Jon Goulding

Contents

Starter test 4

Number – Number and place value

Numbers and counting 12
Counting forwards and backwards 14
Counting in steps of 2, 5 and 10 16
More counting in steps of 2, 5 and 10 18
Counting more and less 20
Place value 22
Less than, greater than and equal to 24

Number – Addition and subtraction

Doubling and halving 26
Solving number problems 28
Using two-digit numbers 30
Solving missing number problems 32
Mixed number problems 34

Progress test 1 36

Number – Multiplication and division

What is multiplication? 40
What is division? 42
2, 5 and 10 times tables – odds and evens 44
Division problems 46
Doubling, halving and dividing 48
Solving multiplication and division problems 50
Numbers all around us 52
More mixed number problems 54

Number – Fractions

Halves as fractions 56
Quarters as fractions 58
Fractions of groups 60
Fractions of numbers 62
Fractions all around us 64

Progress test 2 66

Contents

Measurement
Measuring length and height 70
Measuring weight and capacity 72
Comparing measurements 74
Measuring time 76
Time problems 78
Standard units of money 80
Money problems 82

Geometry – Properties of shapes
2-D shapes 84
3-D shapes 86
Different shapes 88
Progress test 3 90

Geometry – Position and direction
Top, middle and bottom 94
Around, inside and outside 96
Describing positions 98
Left and right turns 100
More position and direction 102
Progress test 4 104
Answers 108
Progress test charts 120

ACKNOWLEDGEMENTS

The author and publisher are grateful to the copyright holders for permission to use quoted materials and images.

All illustrations and images are © Shutterstock.com and © HarperCollinsPublishers

Every effort has been made to trace copyright holders and obtain their permission for the use of copyright material. The author and publisher will gladly receive information enabling them to rectify any error or omission in subsequent editions. All facts are correct at time of going to press.

Without limiting the exclusive rights of any author, contributor or the publisher, any unauthorised use of this publication to train generative artificial intelligence (AI) technologies is expressly prohibited. HarperCollins also exercise their rights under Article 4(3) of the Digital Single Market Directive 2019/790 and expressly reserve this publication from the text and data mining exception.

Published by Collins
An imprint of HarperCollinsPublishers
1 London Bridge Street
London SE1 9GF

HarperCollinsPublishers
Macken House, 39/40 Mayor Street Upper,
Dublin 1, D01 C9W8, Ireland

© HarperCollinsPublishers Limited 2025
ISBN 9780008727796
First published 2025
10 9 8 7 6 5 4 3 2 1

All rights reserved. No part of this publication may be reproduced, stored in a retrieval system, or transmitted, in any form or by any means, electronic, mechanical, photocopying, recording or otherwise, without the prior permission of Collins.

British Library Cataloguing in Publication Data.

A CIP record of this book is available from the British Library.
Publisher: Fiona McGlade
Author: Jon Goulding
Contributor: Alan Dobbs
Project manager and editorial: Katie Galloway
Cover design: Sarah Duxbury
Inside concept design: Ian Wrigley
Text design and layout: Rose & Thorn Creative Services Ltd
Artwork: Shutterstock and Collins
Production: Bethany Brohm
Printed in India by Multivista Global Pvt.Ltd.

MIX
Paper | Supporting responsible forestry
FSC™ C007454

Starter test

1. Fill in the missing numbers. Check which way each set is counting and the steps it counts in.

3 marks

2. What would 1 less and 1 more of each number be? Fill in the boxes.

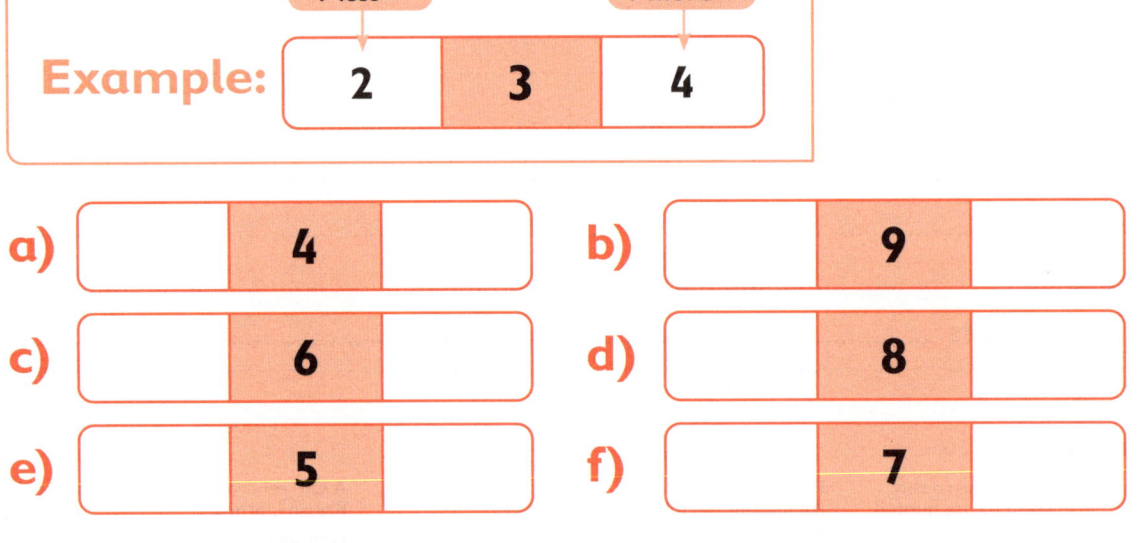

6 marks

3. Tick (✓) the shapes that have $\frac{1}{2}$ coloured.

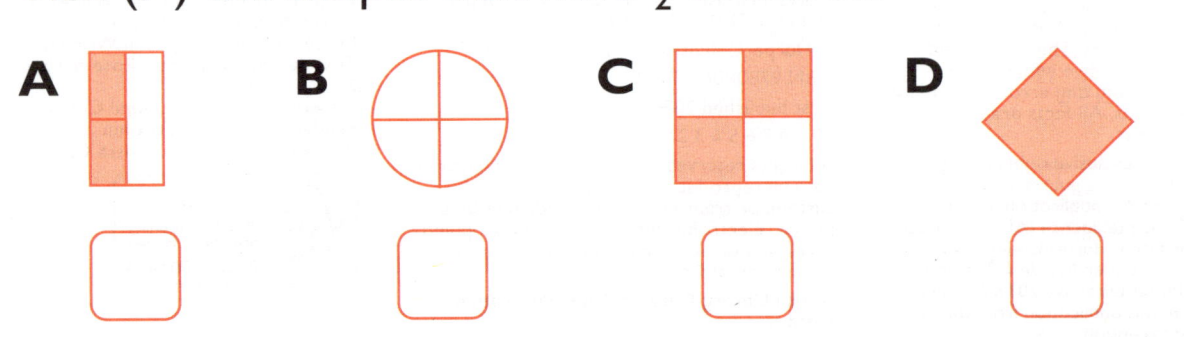

2 marks

4. Draw the correct number of counters to go with each number.

a) 12

b) 17

5. Are these sentences **true** or **false**?

a) When you count in twos, starting at 2, your answer is always an even number. ....

b) If you add an odd number to an even number the answer is always even. ....

c) 3 + 5 has the same total as 5 + 3. ....

6. Write these words as numbers.

Example: Nine ___9___

a) Seven ....

b) Fifteen ....

c) Four ....

d) Twenty ....

e) Seventeen ....

f) Zero ....

7. Sam had a hen and it laid 2 eggs every day.

   a) How many eggs did Sam's hen lay in 3 days? .... eggs

   b) Show how you worked this out.

....

2 marks

8. Write these numbers as words.

Example: 13 _Thirteen_

  a) 12 ....   **b)** 10 ....

  c) 7 ....   **d)** 6 ....

  e) 0 ....   **f)** 14 ....

  g) 11 ....   **h)** 5 ....

  i) 9 ....   **j)** 16 ....

10 marks

9. Nell the pony eats 5 apples every day.

  a) How many apples would she eat in 2 days?

.... apples

  b) How did you work this out?

....

  c) How many apples would she eat in 3 days?

.... apples

  d) How did you work this out?

....

4 marks

10. Circle the calculation in each set that has an error.

a)
1 + 1 = 2
2 + 1 = 3
3 + 1 = 5
4 + 1 = 5

b)
2 + 2 = 6
2 + 4 = 6
2 + 6 = 8
2 + 7 = 9

c)
10 – 5 = 5
12 – 5 = 7
14 – 5 = 10
15 – 5 = 10

3 marks

11. Draw lines to match each time to the correct clock.

a) 3 o'clock   b) 9 o'clock   c) 5 o'clock

3 marks

12. Look at these splendid snakes.

A = 8 cm   B = 15 cm   C = 7 cm   D = 18 cm

a) Which snake is the shortest? ....

b) Is snake A longer or shorter than snake B? ....

c) Which snake is the longest? ....

d) Put the snakes in order from shortest to longest.

shortest [   ] [   ] [   ] [   ] longest

5 marks

Starter test

13. Mia has two biscuits.

   What is half of this amount? ....

14. Write the answer to each problem.

   a)

   8 sets of 2 = ...

   b)

   4 sets of 5 = ...

   c)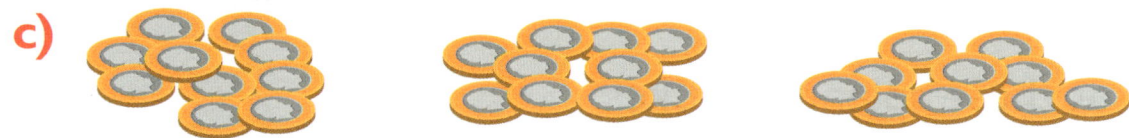

   3 sets of 10 = ...

   d)

   12 sets of 2 = ...

15. Add the following numbers.

   a) 3 + 3 = ...   b) 4 + 4 = ...

   c) 5 + 5 = ...   d) 6 + 6 = ...

16. Look at the busy bees below.

a) Count the bees. How many are there? ....

b) If 2 bees flew away, how many would remain?

....

c) If 3 bees joined the original group, how many would there be now?

....

17. a) Work out if these sequences are correct or incorrect.

Tick (✓) the correct sequences.

A	12	14	16	17	20
B	15	16	17	18	19
C	1	3	5	7	9
D	10	9	8	7	5

b) Describe how these sequences are counting.

A   10 9 8 7 6 5

....

B   2 3 4 5 6

....

c) Tick (✓) the sequence that is the odd one out.

A	5	6	7	8	9	10	☐
B	10	11	12	13	14	15	☐
C	13	12	11	10	9	8	☐

How do you know this?

....

....

2 marks

18. Draw tens and ones counters to show how each of the numbers are split.

One has been done for you.

a) 15

tens	ones
10	1 1 1 1 1

b) 16

tens	ones

c) 29

tens	ones

2 marks

19. Add the flowers.

a)

= .... flowers

b)

= .... flowers

2 marks

20. Draw 10 more counters with each set.

How many are in each set now?

a) 7 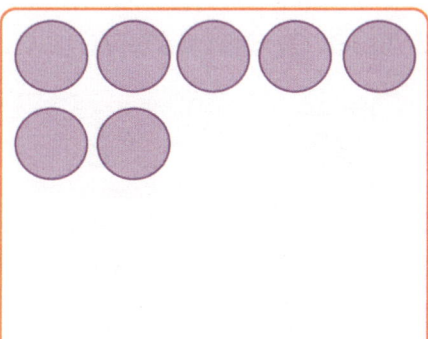   b) 5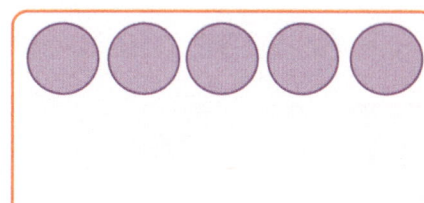

= ....   = ...

2 marks

21. Draw lines to show which item is heaviest and which item is lightest.

| heaviest | | | lightest |

2 marks

How am I doing?   Total marks: ____ / 75

Numbers and counting

Challenge 1

1 a) Circle the number that has the lowest value.

15   11   13   12   14

1 mark

b) Put these numbers in order from lowest to greatest value.

6   3   11   2

lowest [ ] [ ] [ ] [ ] greatest

2 marks

2 a) Tick (✓) the number that has the greatest value.

14   24   22   32   18

1 mark

b) Put the numbers from part **a)** in order from lowest to greatest value.

lowest [ ] [ ] [ ] [ ] [ ] greatest

3 marks

Challenge 2

1. Split these numbers into tens and ones.

   a) 26

tens	ones

   b) 26 = ... + ...

   2 marks

2. a) What is the value of the 1 in 19? ....

   b) What value does the 3 have in 23? ....

   c) What is the value of the 2 in 25? ....

   3 marks

Challenge 3

1. Fill in the missing numbers on this 100 square.

1		3				7	8		
11	12			15					20
		23	24					29	
		33			36				40
41							48		
				55				59	
		63				67			
						77	78		
			84						90
						97			

   10 marks

How am I doing?

Total marks: .... /22

Number – Number and place value

Counting forwards and backwards

Challenge 1

Use this number grid to help you count.

1	2	3	4	5	6	7	8	9	10
11	12	13	14	15	16	17	18	19	20

1 Start at **17** and count **back** the given amounts.

a) Count back 3 = ...

b) Count back 8 = ...

c) Count back 10 = ...

d) Count back 12 = ...

4 marks

2 Start at **3** and count **forwards** the given amounts.

a) Count forwards 4 = ...

b) Count forwards 7 = ...

c) Count forwards 9 = ...

d) Count forwards 12 = ...

4 marks

Challenge 2

1 10 birds are sitting in a tree.

3 of the birds fly away to look for food.

How many birds are still in the tree?   ....

1 mark

14

2 Yusuf collects stickers. He has 12 in his collection. Yusuf gets 5 more stickers.

How many does he have now? ....

1 mark

3 Complete the missing numbers on the number caterpillar.

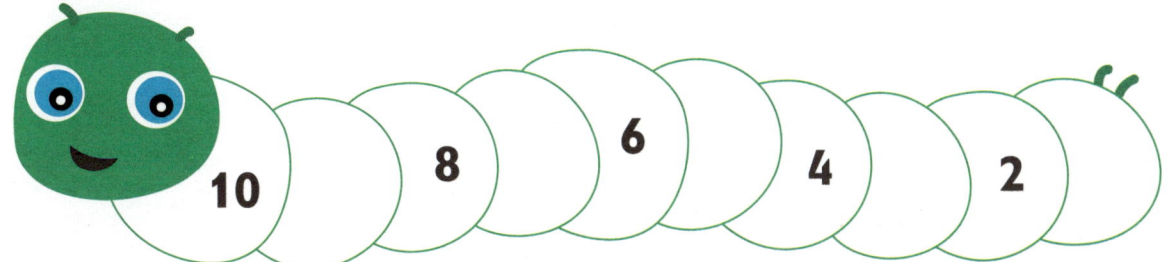

5 marks

Challenge 3

1 Put these numbers in order from greatest to least.

15 14 4 19 5 20 13

greatest [ ][ ][ ][ ][ ][ ][ ] least

5 marks

2 Fill in the empty squares to complete these number grids.

a)
1	2	3
	12	
21		

b)
23	24	25
		35

9 marks

How am I doing? Total marks: [ ] /29

Number – Number and place value

Counting in steps of 2, 5 and 10

Challenge 1

1. Continue the numbers counting in steps of 2. Be careful, they might be counting backwards!

   a) | 2 | 4 | 6 | 8 | | | |

   b) | 15 | 13 | 11 | | | | |

   2 marks

2. What steps are these numbers counting in?

   a) 5 7 9 11

   The numbers are counting in steps of ....

   b) 5 10 15 20

   The numbers are counting in steps of ....

   2 marks

Challenge 2

1. Fill in the blank stepping stones. Count in **steps of 5**!

   a)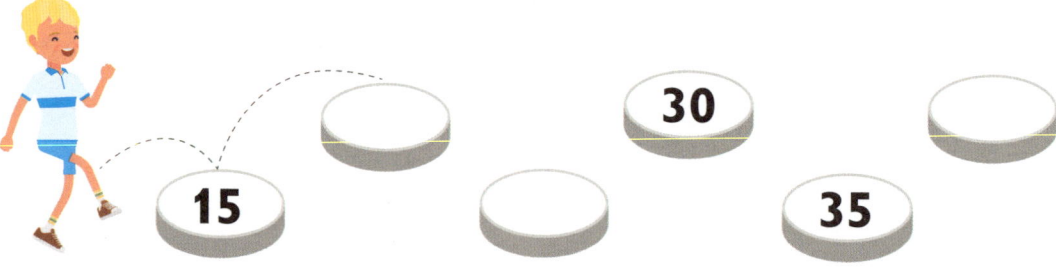

   b)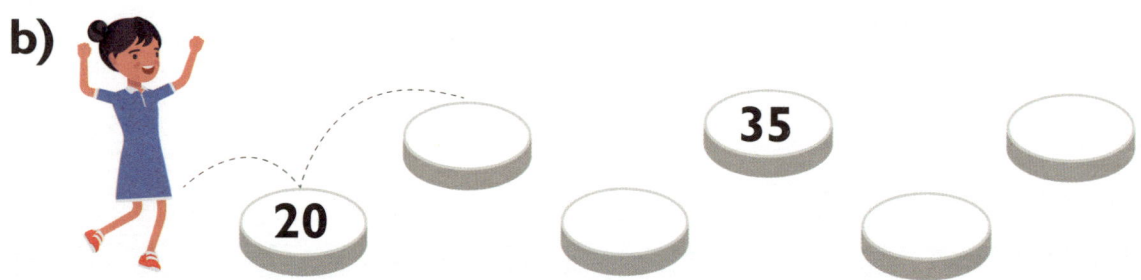

   2 marks

16

2 These numbers are counting in steps of 5, but are they counting **forwards** or **backwards**?

a) 20 15 10 5 0

The numbers are counting ....

b) 14 19 24 29

The numbers are counting ....

2 marks

Challenge 3

1 Fill in the two missing numbers to complete each scarf. You will have to decide what steps they are counting in before you answer.

a)

b)

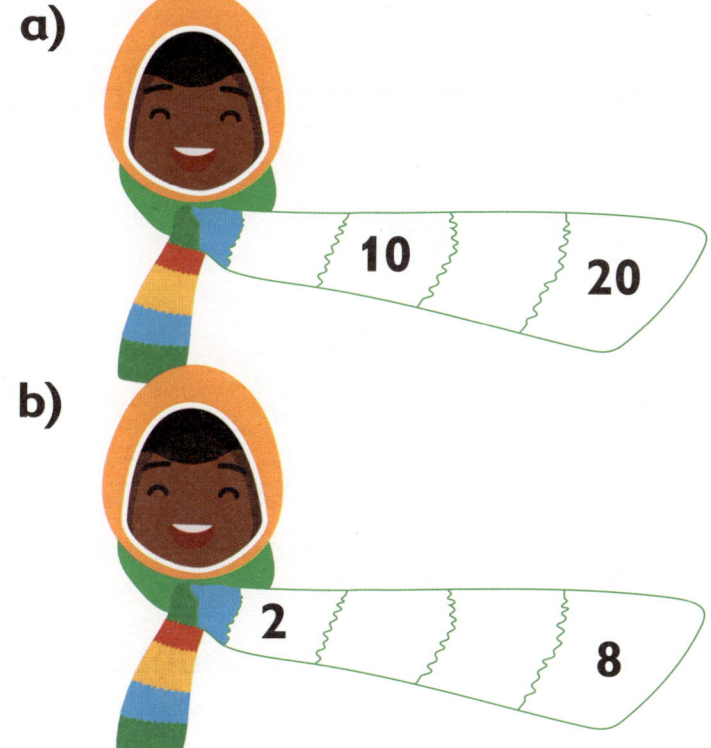

2 marks

2 Is this sentence **true** or **false**?

If I count in steps of 10 starting at 0, the numbers I say will always be even. ....

1 mark

How am I doing?   Total marks: ☐ /11

Number – Number and place value   17

More counting in steps of 2, 5 and 10

Challenge 1

1. Each jar holds 10 sweets. Count the total amount of sweets in lots of 10.

   There are .... sweets in total.

   1 mark

2. How many lots of 10 are there in 20? ....

   1 mark

3. Complete the grid. Make sure you are counting in lots of 10!

	20			50			80

   2 marks

4. Start at 10 and count forwards 3 lots of 10.

   Which number are you at? ....

   1 mark

Challenge 2

1. Put the numbers in order to make a sequence counting **forwards** in **10s**.

   least ⬜ ⬜ ⬜ ⬜ ⬜ greatest

   3 marks

2 Put the numbers in the correct order so they count **forwards** in **10s**.

least ☐ ☐ ☐ ☐ ☐ greatest

3 marks

Challenge 3

1 At school, there are three buses. Each bus has 10 seats.

a) How many **lots of 10** seats are there altogether?

....

b) How many **lots of 5** seats are there altogether?

....

c) How many **lots of 2** seats are there on **1 bus**?

....

d) How many **buses** would you need to have **40 seats**?

....

4 marks

How am I doing?

Total marks: ☐ /15

Number – Number and place value 19

Counting more and less

Challenge 1

1. Find 1 more and 1 less of these numbers.

   a) [___ | 15 | ___]

   b) [___ | 18 | ___]

   c) [___ | 9 | ___]

   d) [___ | 19 | ___]

   e) [___ | 17 | ___]

   5 marks

2. What is 2 more than each number?

   a) 2 ....   b) 4 ....   c) 11 ....

   3 marks

Challenge 2

1. Which of these numbers has a greater value?

   a) 3 or 7? ....   b) 17 or 12? ....

   c) 25 or 19? ....   d) 10 or 15? ....

   4 marks

2. Which of these numbers has a lower value?

   a) 26 or 16? ....   b) 29 or 38? ....

   c) 11 or 16? ....   d) 24 or 27? ....

   4 marks

3. Write the number that is 10 more than 9. ....

   1 mark

Challenge 3

1 What would 10 less than each number be?

a) 14 ....   b) 26 ....

c) 40 ....   d) 32 ....

4 marks

2 Answer these number problems.

a) Arun has **6 gold stars** in his book. Amelia has **4 more** than Arun.

How many stars does Amelia have? ....

b) Jacob has **2 apple trees**. He collects **15 apples** from the first tree. But the second tree has **5 fewer** than the first.

How many apples does the **second tree** have?

....

2 marks

3 Theo takes **20 cupcakes** to school for the summer fair. Ada brings **10 more** than Theo.

a) How many cupcakes does Ada bring? ....

b) How many cupcakes do they both bring in total?

....

Show how you worked this out. ....

3 marks

How am I doing?   Total marks: ____ /26

Number – Number and place value   21

Place value

Challenge 1

1. Write the number that is shown on each abacus.

   a) [tens ones abacus]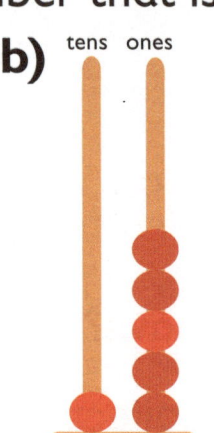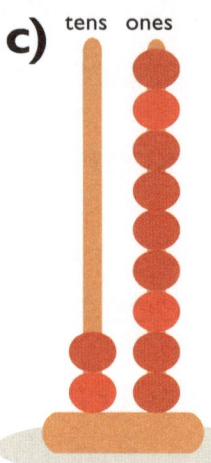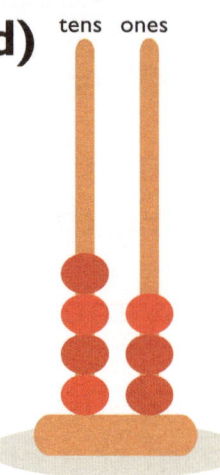

   ....

   4 marks

2. Draw beads on each abacus to show these numbers.

   a) 12 b) 24 c) 35 d) 42

   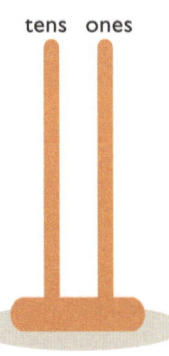 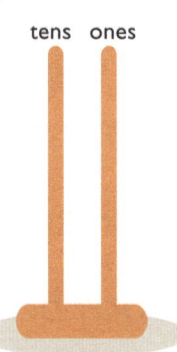 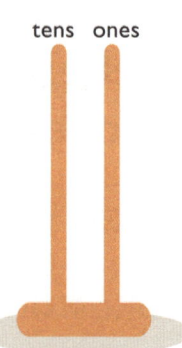 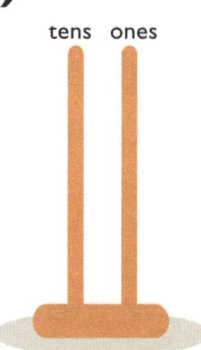

   4 marks

Challenge 2

1. Partition these two-digit numbers into tens and ones.

   Example: 32 = 30 + 2

   a) 12 = ... + ...   b) 25 = ... + ...

   c) 38 = ... + ...   d) 46 = ... + ...

   4 marks

2. Write the two-digit numbers made with these tens and ones.

Example: 50 + 8 = 58

a) 20 + 5 = ...   b) 30 + 1 = ...

c) 40 + 2 = ...   d) 30 + 7 = ...

4 marks

Challenge 3

1. Put these numbers in order from least value to most.

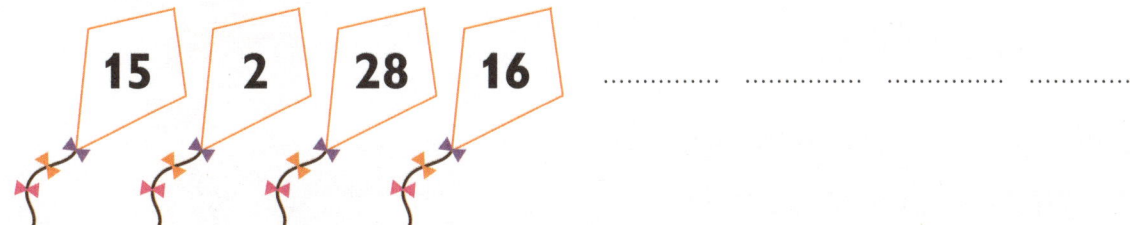

....

2 marks

2. How many tens and ones do these two-digit numbers have?

a) 14: .... ten, ... ones

b) 24: .... tens, ... ones

c) 36: .... tens, ... ones

d) 48: .... tens, ... ones

4 marks

3. This number is between 11 and 15. What could the number be? ....

1 mark

4. There are between 15 and 20 biscuits in this box.

What could be the true number? ....

1 mark

How am I doing?   Total marks: ..../24

Number – Number and place value

Less than, greater than and equal to

Challenge 1

1. Choose from the numbers given to complete the descriptions below.

   (17) (14) (20) (1) (20) (26) (13) (1) (12)

   a) .... is less than ....

   b) .... is greater than ....

   c) .... is equal to ....

    3 marks

2. Choose your own numbers to complete the descriptions.

   a) .... is greater than ....

   b) .... is less than ....

   c) .... is equal to ....

3 marks

Challenge 2

1. Use the words in the boxes to compare the numbers.

   | is less than | is greater than | is equal to |

   Example: 6 is greater than 3

   a) 15 18

   b) 23 23

   c) 20 14

   3 marks

2 Use the words in the boxes to compare the numbers.

| is less than | is greater than | is equal to |

Example: Thirty-five is less than fifty-one

a) Twenty-seven .... thirty-two

b) Twenty-one .... twenty

c) Twenty-six .... twenty-six

3 marks

Challenge 3

1 Choose the correct word from the boxes to make each sentence true.

| fewer | equal | more |

a) If there are 10 pencils and 10 pens, the numbers are ....

b) Albie has 5 badges and Benjamin has 6 badges.

Albie has .... badges than Benjamin.

c) Fran collects 20 blueberries and 15 redcurrants.

She has .... redcurrants than blueberries.

d) 10 fish meet 12 tadpoles. There are .... tadpoles than fish.

4 marks

How am I doing?

Total marks: / 16

Doubling and halving

Challenge 1

1. Draw double the number of counters shown.

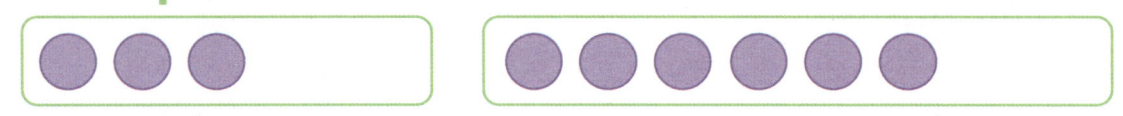

Example:

a)

b)

c)

3 marks

2. Use your answers from Question 1 above to help you complete the following sentences.

a) Double 2 is ....   b) Double 3 is ....

c) Double 4 is ....   d) Double 5 is ....

4 marks

Challenge 2

1. Halve the number of counters shown by crossing out the correct number of counters.

Example:

a)

b)

c)

d)

4 marks

2 Use your answers from Question 1 to help you complete the following sentences.

a) Half of 8 is ....   b) Half of 10 is ....

c) Half of 4 is ....   d) Half of 6 is ....

4 marks

Challenge 3

1 Double and halve these numbers using each set of three cards to help you.

Example: 2, 4, 2   Double 2 is 4, half of 4 = 2

a) [5] [10] [5]   b) [7] [14] [7]

a) Double .... is ...., half of .... = ...

b) Double .... is ...., half of .... = ...

2 marks

2 Now try these numbers without any help!

Example: Double 3 = 3 + 3 = 6

a) Double 2 = ... + ... = ...

b) Double 6 = ... + ... = ...

c) Double 10 = ... + ... = ...

d) Double 8 = ... + ... = ...

4 marks

How am I doing?   Total marks: /21

Number – Addition and subtraction   27

Solving number problems

Challenge 1

1 Answer these addition problems. Draw objects to help you.

a) Max has 7 apples. He then picks 5 more apples. How many apples does Max have in total?

 +

7 + ... = ...

b) Sita has 10 marbles. Her sister gives her 7 more marbles. How many marbles does Sita have altogether?

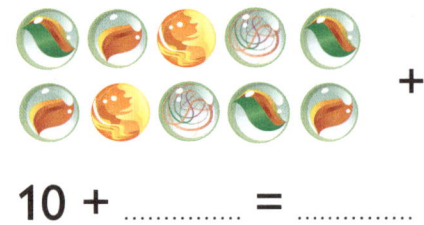 +

10 + ... = ...

c) Zeneb has 5 £1 coins. Her mum gives her another 5 £1 coins for washing the car. How many £1 coins does Zeneb have in total?

 +

5 + ... = ...

3 marks

Challenge 2

1 Answer these subtraction problems. Cross out objects to help you.

a) Amy has 12 frogs in her pond. Three of them hop away. How many frogs are left in the pond?

12 − .... = ...

28

b) Jade finds 10 acorns. She gives 4 of the acorns to her friends. How many acorns does Jade have left?

10 – .... = ...

2 marks

Challenge 3

1. Write the totals of these numbers. Check your answers by adding each set of numbers in a different order.

   a) 5 + 3 + 1

   .... + ... + ... = ...

   .... + ... + ... = ...

   b) 3 + 4 + 2

   .... + ... + ... = ...

   .... + ... + ... = ...

   c) 6 + 1 + 5

   .... + ... + ... = ...

   .... + ... + ... = ...

3 marks

How am I doing?

Total marks: / 8

Using two-digit numbers

Challenge 1

1. Look at the bananas. There are 10 in total. Write eleven addition number facts that total 10.

   Example: 9 + 1 = 10

………… + ………… = 10	
………… + ………… = 10	………… + ………… = 10
………… + ………… = 10	………… + ………… = 10
………… + ………… = 10	………… + ………… = 10
………… + ………… = 10	………… + ………… = 10
………… + ………… = 10	………… + ………… = 10

   11 marks

Challenge 2

1. Create ten different two-digit numbers using the numerals on the cards.

   | 1 | 2 | 5 | 6 | 8 | 3 | 7 | 4 | 9 |

   a) …………   b) …………   c) …………   d) …………   e) …………
   f) …………   g) …………   h) …………   i) …………   j) …………

   10 marks

30

② Add 10 to each of these numbers to change them into two-digit numbers.

a) 3 ....   b) 4 ....   c) 6 ....

d) 1 ....   e) 8 ....

5 marks

Challenge 3

① There are 10 flowers left. Write five subtraction number facts to show how many flowers there could have been to begin with.

Example: 16 − 6 = 10

.... − .... = 10	.... − .... = 10
.... − .... = 10	.... − .... = 10
.... − .... = 10	

5 marks

② These leaves are numbered using two-digit numbers, subtracting 1 each time.

Write the correct numbers on the blank leaves to complete the sequence.

4 marks

How am I doing?   Total marks: ___ /35

Number – Addition and subtraction   31

Solving missing number problems

Challenge 1

1. Use the number grid to complete these additions and subtractions by writing in the missing numbers.

| 1 | 2 | 3 | 4 | 5 | 6 | 7 | 8 | 9 | 10 |

a) 4 + ... = 10

b) 8 − .... = 6

c) 5 + ... = 9

d) 6 − .... = 3

e) 0 + ... = 7

f) 10 − .... = 0

g) 3 + 4 = ...

h) 8 − 6 = ...

8 marks

Challenge 2

1. Use the number grid to complete these additions and subtractions by writing in the missing numbers.

| 1 | 2 | 3 | 4 | 5 | 6 | 7 | 8 | 9 | 10 |
| 11 | 12 | 13 | 14 | 15 | 16 | 17 | 18 | 19 | 20 |

a) 6 + ... = 10

b) 19 − .... = 15

c) .... + 10 = 12

d) 19 + ... = 20

e) 15 − 3 = ...

f) 20 − 8 = ...

g) .... − 4 = 13

h) 16 − .... = 6

8 marks

2 Fill in the missing number operation symbols (− or +).

a) 3 .... 7 = 10

b) 5 .... 10 = 15

c) 15 .... 10 = 5

d) 17 = 10 7

e) 17 = 20 3

5 marks

Challenge 3

1 Casey is selling bows, but she has lost her price tags! She knows that purple bows are 5p. Help Casey to remember the price of her other bows.

a) Pink bows are 3p more than purple bows.

Pink bows cost .... p.

b) Blue bows are 10p more than purple bows.

Blue bows cost .... p.

c) Casey's green bows are 2p more than blue bows.

Green bows cost .... p.

d) Yellow bows cost the same as a pink bow and a blue bow added together.

Yellow bows cost .... p.

e) Orange bows cost 1p less than a purple bow.

Orange bows cost .... p.

5 marks

How am I doing? Total marks: / 26

Number – Addition and subtraction 33

Mixed number problems

Challenge 1

1. True or false? Write **true** or **false** next to these additions.

   a) 12 + 6 = 20 ....

   b) 14 + 6 = 20 ....

   c) 4 + 12 = 15 ....

2. Spot the mistake! Write the correct answer for each addition.

   a) 12 + 7 = 20 ✗   12 + 7 = ...

   b) 15 + 6 = 19 ✗   15 + 6 = ...

   c) 3 + 12 = 16 ✗   3 + 12 = ...

Challenge 2

1. a) Alex is thinking of a number. The number is 10 less than 25.

      What is Alex's number? ....

   b) Maryam is thinking of a number between 14 and 21. Write the possible numbers that Maryam could be thinking of.

      ....

   c) Dan and Sian both have a number. Sian's number is 10 more than Dan's. Dan's number is 12.

      What is Sian's number? ....

   d) Adam has 10 stickers. He gives 5 stickers away.

      How many stickers does Adam have left? ....

Challenge 3

1. Put a tick (✓) next to the correct subtractions, and a cross (✗) next to the ones that are wrong.

   a) 13 − 7 = 6 ☐   b) 20 − 12 = 8 ☐

   c) 12 − 5 = 6 ☐

   3 marks

2. a) Myles has 12 pumpkins. He gives 5 to Syed. How many pumpkins does Myles have left? ....

   b) Write the subtraction that shows this.

   .... − .... = ...

   2 marks

3. Write **true** or **false** next to these statements.

   a) If you subtract a smaller number from a greater number the total is always less. ....

   b) Subtracting an odd number from an even number always gives you an even number. ....

   2 marks

4. a) Harry subtracted 10 from his starting number. His answer was 10. What was Harry's starting number? ....

   1 mark

   b) Kira's answer is 5. Write four subtractions that she could have made.

   .... − .... = 5   .... − .... = 5

   .... − .... = 5   .... − .... = 5

   4 marks

How am I doing?   **Total marks:** ☐ /22

Progress test 1

1. Double these numbers.

   a) 5 ....   b) 4 ....

   c) 10 ....   d) 6 ....

   4 marks

2. What is half of each number?

   a) 2 ....   b) 4 ....

   c) 10 ....   d) 20 ....

   4 marks

3. Put any two of these numerals together to form eight different two-digit numbers.

   > **Example:** **1** and **3** make the two-digit number **13**

   ....

   8 marks

4. a) Rob counts 3 butterflies in his garden. He sees 4 more. How many butterflies can Rob now see?

   ....

   b) Three of the butterflies fly away. How many butterflies can Rob see now? ....

   c) Six new butterflies appear. What is the total number of butterflies now? ....

   3 marks

5. Swap the order of the numbers being added to make equal addition facts.

   a) 9 + 3 = 12 ....

   b) 2 + 8 = 10 ....

   c) 7 + 4 = 11 ....

6. Circle the card that has the highest value.

7. Write these numbers using digits.

   a) Seven ....   b) Fourteen ....

   c) Sixteen ....   d) Twenty ....

8. Tom has some large marbles and some small marbles. The large marbles each have a value of 10 and the small marbles are 1s. What numbers has Tom made using the marbles?

   a)  ....

   b)  ....

   c)  ....

9. What is 5 less than each number?

   a) 9 ....   b) 10 ....

   c) 20 ....   d) 16 ....

10. Write these numbers as words.

a) 5 .... b) 7 ....

c) 9 .... d) 2 ....

e) 12 ....

5 marks

11. Complete this addition grid. Make sure that each **column** and each **row** has a total of 10. You could use objects to help you.

1	5	
1		6
	2	0

3 marks

12. Look at the cards below.

| 1 | 2 | 5 | 6 | 8 | 3 | 7 | 4 | 9 |

a) Using any two numbers from the cards, what is the lowest value, two-digit number possible? ....

b) Using any two numbers from the cards, what is the highest value two-digit number possible? ....

c) Make an **odd** two-digit number from the numbers on the cards. ....

d) Make an **even** two-digit number from the numbers on the cards. ....

4 marks

13. Find the fact families for these sets of numbers.

> **Example:** 13, 7, 20 gives 13 + 7 = 20, 7 + 13 = 20,
> 20 − 7 = 13, 20 − 13 = 7

a) 14, 5, 19

.... + ... = ... + ... = ...

.... − .... = ... − .... = ...

b) 11, 4, 15

.... + ... = ... + ... = ...

.... − .... = ... − .... = ...

14. Draw circles around the stars to put them into groups of 5.

15. Shen has 7 toy cars. He wins 6 more.

How many cars does Shen have now? ....

How am I doing?   Total marks: ☐ / 50

What is multiplication?

Challenge 1

1 Use the buttons to answer the questions.

a) Count the holes in lots of 2.

There are .... holes in total.

b) Write this as a multiplication.

.... sets of 2 = ...

2 marks

2 Write the multiplication for each of these additions.

a) 2 + 2 + 2 = 6   .... sets of .... = ...

b) 5 + 5 = 10   .... sets of .... = ...

c) 10 + 10 + 10 = 30   .... sets of .... = ...

3 marks

Challenge 2

1 There are two possible multiplications shown by this array of blocks. What are they?

.... sets of .... = ...

.... sets of .... = ...

2 marks

40

2 Draw blocks to show each of these multiplications.

a) 4 sets of 2	b) 3 sets of 5	c) 2 sets of 10

6 marks

Challenge 3

1 Complete the table. The first row has been done for you.

Addition	Number of sets
2 + 2 + 2 + 2 + 2 = 10	5 sets of 2
	3 sets of 5
10 + 10 + 10 = 30	
	4 sets of 5
	5 sets of 10
2 + 2 + 2 + 2 + 2 + 2 = 12	

5 marks

How am I doing?   Total marks: ☐ /18

Number – Multiplication and division   41

What is division?

Challenge 1

1 Answer these division problems. Use objects to help you.

a) There are 4 crayons to share equally between 2 people. How many crayons will each person get?

Each person will get .... crayons.

b) If you share 6 pencils between two people, how many will each person get?

Each person will get .... pencils.

c) If you share 10 books between two people, how many will each person get?

Each person will get .... books.

3 marks

Challenge 2

1 Share these raspberries equally between 2 people.

Each person will get .... raspberries.

1 mark

② Here are 2 hungry children! Share 12 apple slices equally between the 2 children.

Each child will get .... apple slices.

③ Share 9 oranges equally between 3 people.

Each person will get .... oranges.

1 mark

1 mark

Challenge 3

① Complete this table by sharing the number of items between the number of people. The first row has been done for you. Use counters to help you.

Number of items	Number of people	They each get
6	2	3
14	2	
16	2	
18	2	
20	2	

4 marks

How am I doing?   Total marks: ☐ /10

Number – Multiplication and division 43

2, 5 and 10 times tables – odds and evens

Challenge 1

1. Complete this grid showing the 2, 5 and 10 times tables by writing the answers and drawing the counters. The first row and some of the counters have been done for you.

2 times 1 = 2 ● ●	5 times 1 = 5 ● ● ● ● ●	10 times 1 = 10 ● ● ● ● ● ● ● ● ● ●
2 times 2 = ... ● ● ● ●	5 times 2 = ...	10 times 2 = ...
2 times 3 = ... ● ● ● ● ● ●	5 times 3 = ... ● ● ● ● ● ● ● ● ● ● ● ● ● ● ●	10 times 3 = ...

9 marks

Challenge 2

1. Colour in the odd numbers and circle the even numbers. One column has been done for you.

1	2	3	4	5
6	7	8	9	10
11	12	13	14	15
16	17	18	19	20

4 marks

2 Is each sentence **true** or **false**?

a) When you count in 2s, starting from 2, the numbers you say are sometimes **odd numbers**.

....

b) When you count in 2s, starting from 2, the numbers you say are always **even numbers**.

....

2 marks

Challenge 3

Multiplication is **commutative**. It has the same **product** even if the order of the **numbers** is changed.

Example: 3 times 2 = 6 and 2 times 3 = 6

1 Write the **commutative** of each multiplication.

a) 4 times 2 = 8 and ....

b) 1 times 10 = 10 and ....

2 marks

2 Each **array** shows two **multiplications**. Write the two multiplications shown by each array.

a)    **b)**

....

....

4 marks

How am I doing?   Total marks: ☐ / 21

Number – Multiplication and division

Division problems

Challenge 1

1 Look at the strawberries.

There are 6 strawberries split into 2 groups of 3.

Write down the division that you can see.

.... shared by 2 = ...

1 mark

2 Use each set of numbers to write a correct division.

a) 10   2   5   .... shared by .... = ...

b) 20   10   2   .... shared by .... = ...

c) 16   2   8   .... shared by .... = ...

3 marks

3 Rearrange each set of numbers to make a correct division. Be careful, they are tricky!

a) 9   18   2   .... shared by .... = ...

b) 2   4   8   .... shared by .... = ...

c) 12   6   2   .... shared by .... = ...

3 marks

46

Challenge 2

1 Tao has grown 20 sunflowers. He wants to share them with his friends.

a) If the sunflowers are shared between 2 friends, how many will they get each? ....

b) Write this as a division.

.... shared by .... = ...

c) If 4 friends share the sunflowers, they would get .... each.

3 marks

Challenge 3

1 The coins below show three different ways that Jessica could have **20p**. Complete the sentences.

a) 20p is equal to .... 10p coins.

b)  20p is equal to .... 5p coins.

c)

20p is equal to .... 2p coins.

3 marks

How am I doing?   Total marks: ☐ / 13

Number – Multiplication and division   47

Doubling, halving and dividing

Challenge 1

1) Multiply these numbers by 2 to double them.

   Example: Double 4 is 8

   a) ⬤⬤⬤⬤⬤ Double 5 is ....

   b) ⬤⬤⬤⬤⬤⬤⬤⬤⬤⬤ Double 10 is ....

   c) ⬤⬤⬤ Double 3 is ....

   3 marks

2) Now divide these numbers by 2 to halve them.

   Example: Half of 10 is 5

   a) ⬤⬤⬤⬤ Half of 4 is ....

   b) ⬤⬤⬤⬤⬤⬤⬤⬤ Half of 8 is ....

   c) ⬤⬤⬤⬤⬤⬤⬤⬤⬤⬤ Half of 10 is ....

   3 marks

Challenge 2

1) Count these busy bees.

   a) How many bees are there in total? ....

   b) How many bees would half of this amount be? ....

   2 marks

2 Now count these flowers.

a) How many flowers are there in total?

....

b) How many flowers would there be if you doubled them?   ....

Draw how many flowers there would be in total if you doubled them.

2 marks

Challenge 3

1 Count these apples and then answer the questions that follow.

a) How many groups of 2 are there?   ....

b) How many groups of 10 are there?   ....

c) How many groups of 5 are there?   ....

d) How many groups of 20 are there?   ....

4 marks

How am I doing?   Total marks:  /14

Number – Multiplication and division   49

Solving multiplication and division problems

Challenge 1

1 Ravi had a hen and it laid 1 egg every day.

   a) How many eggs did Ravi's hen lay in 5 days? ....

   b) How many eggs did Ravi's hen lay in 10 days? ....

2 marks

2 Henry had 2 pizzas. He cut them into quarters.

   a) How many slices of pizza did Henry have in total? ....

   b) Henry ate half of the full amount. How many slices of pizza did he eat? ....

2 marks

Challenge 2

1 This is sports club!

   a) Count how many children are in the club.

   There are .... children.

50

b) Each child runs with a partner. How many pairs of two can you count? ....

c) How many lots of 5 is this? ....

3 marks

2 Amir had 5 pens. Libby had double the amount.

a) How many pens did Libby have? ....

b) How many lots of 5 did Amir and Libby have in total? ....

2 marks

Challenge 3

2 Complete the table by answering the problems. The first one has been done for you.

	Number problem	Answer
	One bike has 2 wheels. How many wheels do 4 bikes have?	8 wheels
a)	Two ladybirds have 8 spots. How many spots does 1 ladybird have?	
b)	There are 10 boys in Year 1. Year 2 has double the amount of boys. How many boys are in Year 2?	
c)	Sati gets 10 stickers each week. How many stickers will she get in 3 weeks?	

3 marks

How am I doing?

Total marks: .... / 12

Number – Multiplication and division 51

Numbers all around us

Challenge 1

1 Beth and Evie live on this street.

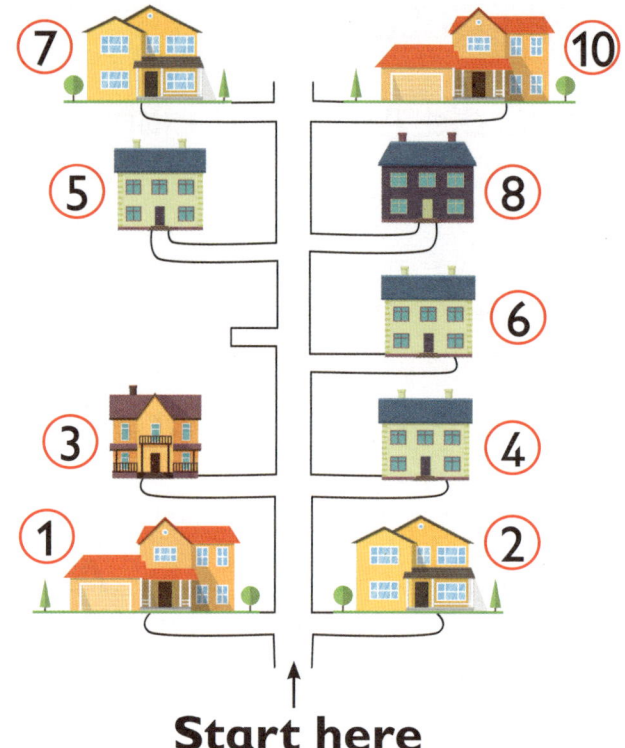

Start here

a) Beth lives at number 4. Evie lives opposite Beth.

   What is the number of Evie's house? ....

b) Their friend Teddy lives at the third house on the right.

   What is the number of Teddy's house? ....

c) Evie's gran lives at number 7.

   Which house is opposite her gran's house? ....

d) Do the houses on the right have odd or
   even numbers? ....

e) Do the houses on the left have odd or
   even numbers? ....

5 marks

Challenge 2

1 There are 10 children on a school bus.

a) 6 children get off at the first stop. How many children are still on the bus? ....

b) More children get on and the bus has 10 again. Of the 10 children, 5 are girls. How many boys are on the bus? ....

c) At the next stop, 3 children get off the bus. How many children are left on the bus? ....

3 marks

Challenge 3

1 Nancy has 20 sweets in a bag.

a) 5 of the sweets are red. How many are **not** red? ....

Show how you worked this out as a subtraction.

.... − .... = ...

2 marks

b) 10 sweets are yellow. The rest of the sweets are green. How many sweets are green? (Don't forget the red sweets!) ....

1 mark

c) Nancy shares the sweets with her friend. How many sweets do they get each? ....

1 mark

How am I doing?   Total marks: ☐ /12

Number – Multiplication and division

More mixed number problems

Challenge 1

1. How many sets of 2 are there in the groups of cars?

   a) = ... sets of 2.

   b) = ... sets of 2.

   c)

   = ... sets of 2.

   3 marks

Challenge 2

1. Share the pencils below equally between 2 people.

   Each person would get .... pencils.

   1 mark

2. Fill in the blanks to complete these sentences.

   a) 8 shared by 2 equals ....

   b) 10 shared by 2 equals ....

   c) 12 shared by 2 equals ....

   3 marks

3 Write **true** or **false** next to these statements.

a) If you share 20 between 2 people, they must each get different amounts. ....

b) You can share an even number between 2 equally. ....

2 marks

Challenge 3

1 Fill in the missing numbers.

a)  = ...

b) The addition above can be written as:

.... groups of .... = ...

2 marks

2 Fill in the missing numbers.

a)  = ...

b) The addition above can be written as:

.... groups of .... = ...

2 marks

3 True or false? Tick (✓) the **true** multiplications and put a cross (✗) next to the ones that are **false**.

a) 2 times 5 = 10   ☐   b) 5 times 10 = 30   ☐

c) 5 times 2 = 12   ☐   d) 4 times 5 = 20   ☐

4 marks

How am I doing?   Total marks: ☐ /17

Number – Multiplication and division

Halves as fractions

Challenge 1

1. For each shape, put a tick (✓) in the box if $\frac{1}{2}$ is shaded or a cross (✗) in the box if $\frac{1}{2}$ is not shaded.

a)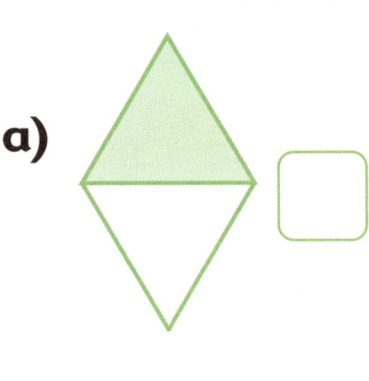

b)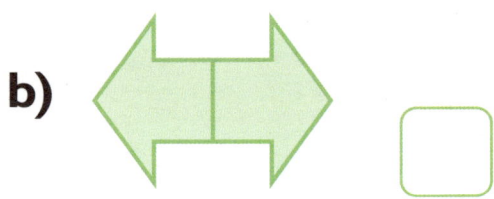

c)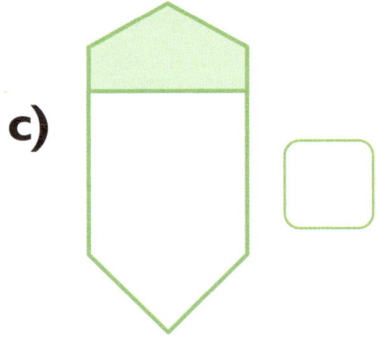

d)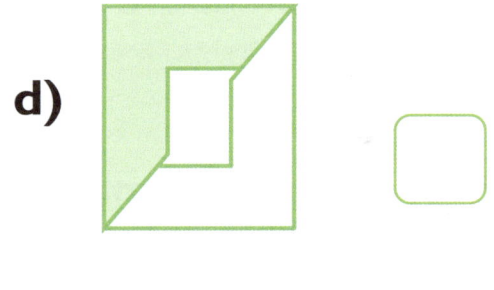

e)

f)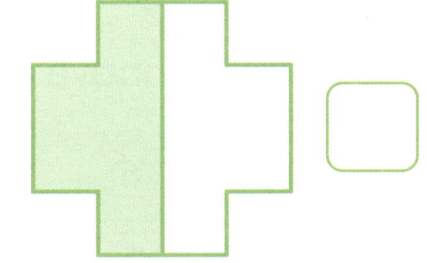

6 marks

56

Challenge 2

1. Shade in one half of each circle.

   a)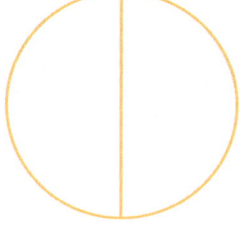

   b)

   c)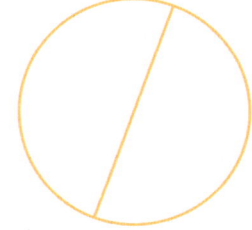

   d)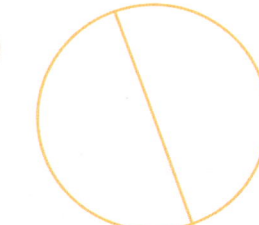

   4 marks

2. How many halves are there in 2 circles? ....

   1 mark

Challenge 3

1. Shade one half of each square.

   a)

   b)

   c)

   d)

   4 marks

2. How many halves are there in 4 squares? ....

   1 mark

How am I doing?

Total marks: / 16

Number – Fractions

Quarters as fractions

Challenge 1

1. Tick (✓) the shapes that have $\frac{1}{4}$ shaded.

    A   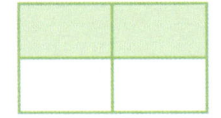 B    C

   2 marks

2. Look at these shapes. They are divided into four equal parts. Colour $\frac{1}{4}$ of each shape.

   a)    b)    c)    d)

   4 marks

3. Now colour $\frac{1}{4}$ of each of these shapes.

   a)    b)    c)    d)

   4 marks

Challenge 2

1. Tick (✓) the shapes that have $\frac{1}{4}$ shaded and put a cross (✗) next to the ones that have $\frac{1}{2}$ shaded.

   a)

   b)

c)  ☐   d)  ☐

e)  ☐

5 marks

Challenge 3

1 Each pizza is cut into quarters. How much of each pizza is left? Draw lines to match each fraction with the correct pizza.

a)    b) 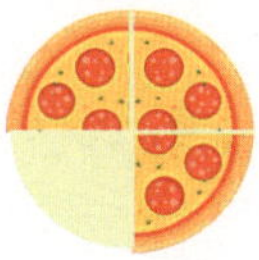   c)    d)    e)

| 1 quarter | 2 quarters | 3 quarters | 0 quarters | 4 quarters |

5 marks

2 Look again at the pizzas. How many quarters of each pizza have been eaten?

a) .... b) .... c) ....

d) .... e) ....

5 marks

How am I doing?   Total marks: ☐ /25

Number – Fractions   59

Fractions of groups

Challenge 1

1. Look at these groups of buttons.

   A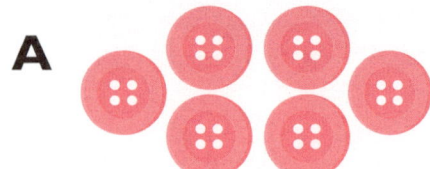

   B

   C

   D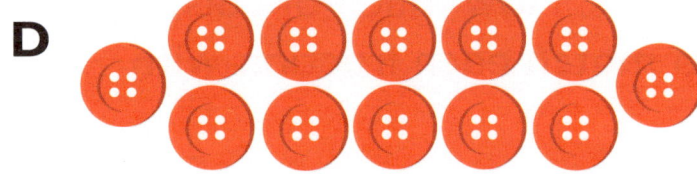

   a) Draw a circle around $\frac{1}{2}$ of group A. How many buttons have you circled? ....

   b) Draw a circle around $\frac{1}{2}$ of group B. How many buttons have you circled? ....

   c) Circle $\frac{1}{2}$ of group C. How many buttons have you circled? ....

   d) How many buttons are in $\frac{1}{2}$ of group D? ....

   e) How many buttons are in $\frac{1}{4}$ of group B? ....

   5 marks

Challenge 2

1 Look at the group of shells and answer the questions.

a) Draw a red line around $\frac{1}{4}$ of the shells.

How many shells have you drawn around? ....

b) Draw a blue line around half of the shells.

How many shells have you drawn around? ....

c) How many sets of 4 shells can you make from the whole group? ....

3 marks

Challenge 3

1 Complete the table by working out the fractions.

Items	Amount in $\frac{1}{4}$	Amount in $\frac{1}{2}$
4 stickers		
20 buns		
8 straws		
12 apples		

8 marks

How am I doing?   Total marks: ☐ / 16

Number – Fractions   61

Fractions of numbers

Challenge 1

1 Write the numbers that make these sentences correct.

a) $\frac{1}{2}$ of 2 is ....   b) $\frac{1}{2}$ of 6 is ....

c) $\frac{1}{4}$ of 4 is ....   d) $\frac{1}{4}$ of 8 is ....

4 marks

2 Draw lines to show which fraction is greater and which is smaller.

$\frac{1}{2}$ $\frac{1}{4}$

smaller   greater

1 mark

Challenge 2

1 Write the numbers that make these sentences correct.

a) $\frac{1}{2}$ of 12 is ....

b) $\frac{1}{4}$ of 12 is ....

c) $\frac{1}{2}$ of 16 is ....

d) $\frac{1}{2}$ of 10 is ....

e) $\frac{1}{4}$ of 20 is ....

5 marks

2 Are these sentences **true** or **false**?

a) $\frac{1}{2}$ of 10 is 6 ....

b) $\frac{1}{4}$ of 20 is 5 ....

c) $\frac{1}{2}$ of 16 is 8 ....

d) $\frac{1}{4}$ of 16 is 3 ....

e) $\frac{1}{2}$ of 18 is 9 ....

5 marks

Challenge 3

1 Have a go at these fraction questions.

a) A quarter of this number is 2. What is the number?

....

b) Half of this number is 10. What is the number?

....

c) A quarter of the number equals 5. What is the whole number? ....

d) Half of this number is 3. What is the number?

....

e) $\frac{1}{4}$ of this number equals 4. What is the number?

....

5 marks

How am I doing?   Total marks: ____ / 20

Fractions all around us

Challenge 1

1 Oliver empties his money box. These are the coins he has.

a) How many coins does Oliver have?

   Oliver has .... coins.

b) Amy has half the amount of coins. How many coins does Amy have?

   Amy has .... coins.

c) Some of Oliver's coins are 2p coins. What is half of 2p?

   Half of 2p is .... p.

3 marks

Challenge 2

1 This is Tomas's fish tank.

64

a) How many fish does Tomas have in total? ....

b) Half of the fish are pink.

   How many fish are pink? ....

c) Half of the fish are yellow.

   How many fish are yellow? ....

d) What would be a quarter of the total number of fish? ....

4 marks

Challenge 3

1. Razz, Evan and Deli have had a snail race!
   Evan's snail came first and travelled 12 cm in 12 minutes.

a) Razz's snail only went half the distance of Evan's.

   Razz's snail travelled .... cm.

b) Deli's snail went a quarter of 12 cm. How far did Deli's snail go? .... cm

c) Evan's snail travelled 1 cm every minute. How far had his snail travelled after 2 minutes? .... cm

d) How far had Evan's snail gone after 4 minutes?

   .... cm

4 marks

How am I doing?   Total marks: ☐ /11

Number – Fractions   65

Progress test 2

1. Solve these addition problems.

   a) 3 + 6 = ...   b) 10 + 5 = ...

   c) 7 + 4 = ...   d) 9 + 2 = ...

   4 marks

2. Partition each two-digit number into tens and ones.

   a) 27 = ... tens, ... ones

   b) 19 = ... ten, ... ones

   c) 21 = ... tens, ... one

   d) 25 = ... tens, ... ones

   e) 15 = ... ten, ... ones

   5 marks

3. Find the fractions.

   a) How many would half of these sweets be?

   ....

   b) How many sweets would there be in $\frac{1}{4}$ of this group?

   ....

   c) How many sweets are there all together? ....

   3 marks

4. Find half of each number by dividing.

   a) Half of sixteen is ....

   b) Half of twenty is ....

   c) Half of 8 is ....

   d) Half of 10 is ....

   e) Half of 14 is ....

5 marks

5. Double each number by multiplying.

   a) Double 2 is ....

   b) Double 5 is ....

   c) Double 10 is ....

   d) Double 8 is ....

   e) Double 7 is ....

5 marks

6. Colour these arrays to show the following calculations.

   a) 4 times 2 = 8   **b)** 5 times 2 = 10

2 marks

7. Hopscotch the rabbit eats 2 carrots every day. How many carrots would he eat in:

   a) 2 days? ....

   b) 5 days? ....

   c) 10 days? ....

3 marks

Progress test 2   67

8. Count up using 5s to complete the flowerpots.

4 marks

9. Show 1 more and 1 less than each number.

a) | 1 less = | 13 | 1 more = |

b) | 1 less = | 11 | 1 more = |

c) | 1 less = | 19 | 1 more = |

3 marks

10. Use the words in the boxes to make each number sentence correct.

| is less than | is greater than | is equal to |

a) 8 5

b) 7 17

c) 19 18

d) 16 16

e) 10 11

5 marks

11. Add the numbers. Check your answers by adding in a different order.

a) 3 + 5

.... + ... = ...

.... + ... = ...

b) 3 + 2 + 1

.... + ... + ... = ...

.... + ... + ... = ...

12. Find the fractions of these groups of plums.

A

B

C

a) How many plums are in $\frac{1}{4}$ of group A? ....

b) How many plums are in $\frac{1}{4}$ of group B? ....

c) How many plums are in $\frac{1}{2}$ of group C? ....

d) How many plums are in $\frac{1}{2}$ of group A? ....

Measuring length and height

Challenge 1

1. Look at the picture below.

Put the objects in order from the tallest to the shortest. The first one has been done for you.

tallest | B | | | | | shortest

4 marks

Challenge 2

1. Draw lines to match the items to their heights.

| about 1 m | less than 1 m | about 3 m | over 5 m | less than 1 m |

5 marks

2. Use a cm ruler to measure these straws.

a)  = ... cm

b) = ... cm

2 marks

Challenge 3

1. These caterpillars are different lengths.

   A = 5 cm   B = 10 cm   C = 8 cm   D = 12 cm

   a) Which caterpillar is the **longest**? ....

   b) Which caterpillar is the **shortest**? ....

   c) Is caterpillar C **longer** or **shorter** than caterpillar D? ....

   d) Put the caterpillars into **letter** order from shortest to longest.

   ....

   e) How long would caterpillars **A** and **B** be together?

   .... cm

   6 marks

2.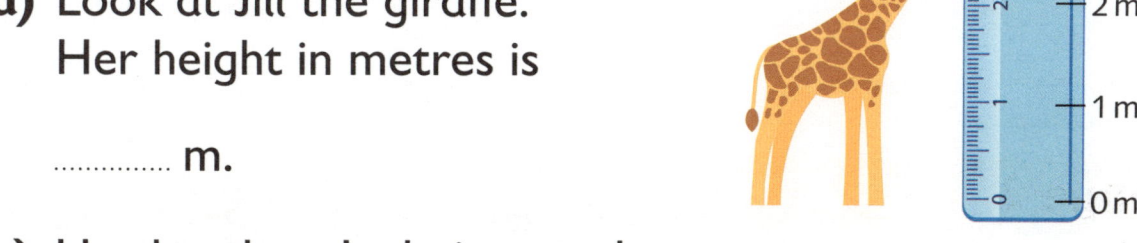

   a) Look at Jill the giraffe. Her height in metres is .... m.

   b) Her brother, Jack, is exactly 1 m smaller than Jill. How tall is Jack? .... m

   c) Jill has a baby called Jem. Jem is **half** the height of Jack. What is the height of Jem? .... m

   d) Jill's dad Ginger is 5 metres from head to hoof! How much taller is Ginger than Jill? .... m

   4 marks

How am I doing?   Total marks: ....../21

Measurement   71

Measuring weight and capacity

Challenge 1

3 Look at the items and their weights.

A	B	C	D
20 g	100 g	Over 500 g	200 g

a) Which item weighs the least? Circle the correct letter.

b) Which item weighs the most? Circle the correct letter.

c) Write the items in order from **lightest** to **heaviest**.

....

4 marks

Challenge 2

1 These bottles contain different amounts of juice.

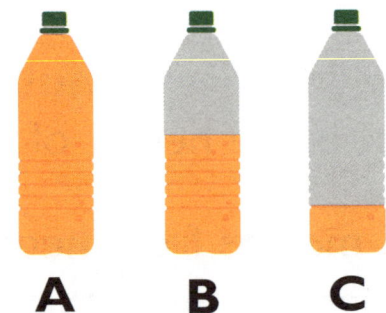

A   B   C

a) Put the bottles in order from **smallest** to **largest** volume of juice.   ....

b) Bottle A contains 2 litres of juice. Which bottle contains about 1 litre of juice? Circle the correct letter.

A   B   C

c) If all three bottles were full, how much would they contain in total? Tick (✓) your answer.

3 litres ☐   6 litres ☐   10 litres ☐

3 marks

Challenge 3

1 Some friends have been collecting strawberries.

Fred = 1 kg   **Ali = 2 kg**   **Susie = 2 kg**   **Ruby = 3 kg**

a) Who collected the **most**? ....

b) Who collected the **least**? ....

c) Which two friends collected **equal** amounts?

.... and ....

d) Who collected the **same amount** as Ali and Fred added together? ....

e) Put the weights in order from **heaviest** to **lightest**.

....

6 marks

How am I doing?   Total marks: ☐ / 13

Measurement 73

Comparing measurements

Challenge 1

1 Lukas, Eric and Bella planted three sunflowers. They have all started to grow. Complete the sentences describing the sunflowers.

   A Lukas   **B Eric**   **C Bella**

a) Lukas's sunflower is .... than Bella's.

b) The tallest sunflower belongs to ....

c) Eric's sunflower is the ....

d) The three sunflowers measure 15 cm, 20 cm and 30 cm. The 20 cm sunflower belongs to ....

4 marks

Challenge 2

1 Carly wants to fill a paddling pool for her pet dog Hogan.

a) Carly has a 1 litre jug and the pool holds 10 litres.

How many jugs of water will she need? ....

74

b) Carly's friend Louie has a pool that holds twice the volume of water. How many litres of water will Louie's pool hold? .... litres

c) If you combined both pools, what would be the volume of water? .... litres

d) How many 10 litre buckets would that be? ....

4 marks

Challenge 3

1 Ade has entered a pumpkin competition.

A = 5 kg **B = 4 kg** **C = 1 kg**

a) Ade's pumpkin is heavier than Chang's and lighter than Katie's.

Is Ade's pumpkin A, B or C? ....

b) Katie's pumpkin weighs 1 kg more than Ade's.

Katie's pumpkin weighs .... kg.

c) Chang's pumpkin is the lightest.

How much lighter is Chang's pumpkin than Ade's?

.... kg

d) Which pumpkins are equal to Katie's when added together? .... and ....

4 marks

How am I doing?   Total marks: ☐ /12

Measurement 75

Measuring time

Challenge 1

1. Use the grid to help you answer these questions.

Monday	Tuesday	Wednesday	Thursday
Friday	Saturday	Sunday	

a) Which day is 1 day after Tuesday? ....

b) Which day is 3 days before Friday? ....

c) If tomorrow is Thursday and yesterday was Tuesday, what day is it today? ....

3 marks

2. Look at the months – they are not in the right order. Write them in the correct order.

January	March	June	February
April	December	August	October
July	November	May	September

....

....

....

....

3 marks

Challenge 2

1 Draw lines to match the correct times to the clocks.

a)  b)  c)  d)  e)

| 5 o'clock | 2 o'clock | half past 8 | 3 o'clock | half past 4 |

5 marks

Challenge 3

1 Draw the minute and hour hands on these clock faces to show the times.

a) 1 o'clock b) 4 o'clock c) Half past 2

d) Half past 5 e) 7 o'clock f) Half past 11

6 marks

How am I doing?   Total marks: /17

Measurement 77

Time problems

Challenge 1

1 Put these events in order from the earliest to the latest.

have lunch	go to bed	wake up	go to school	have breakfast
A	B	C	D	E

Write the letters to show the correct order.

....

3 marks

2 Choose words from the cards to make these sentences true.

first	after	next	before

a) Squeeze on the toothpaste .... you brush your teeth.

b) Wash the plates .... dinner.

c) .... get dressed and then put on your shoes.

d) First pour in the juice. .... pour in the water.

4 marks

Challenge 2

1 Choose words from the cards to make the sentences correct. Be careful, not all of the words are needed!

morning	evening	today	tomorrow

78

a) If it is the twelfth now, then .... is the thirteenth.

b) I always wake up early in the ....

c) Every .... after school, I play with my friends.

3 marks

2 Circle the correct words.

a) 10 years is a **century** / **decade**.

b) There are 31 **days** / **weeks** in most months.

2 marks

Challenge 3

1 Each day Lucy takes her dog Peg out for a walk. She sets off at 11 o'clock (shown on clock A) and walks for 2 hours.

A   B

a) Draw the time that Lucy and Peg get back home from their walk on clock B.

b) What time is it when Lucy and Peg have been walking for 1 hour? .... o'clock

c) How many hours would Lucy and Peg walk in two days? .... hours

3 marks

How am I doing?   Total marks: / 15

Measurement   79

Standard units of money

Challenge 1

1. Look at the coins below.

   a) How many coins are there in total? ....

   b) What is the total value of the coins? .... p

   2 marks

2. Look at the coins below.

   a) How many coins are there in total? ....

   b) What is the total value of the coins? .... p

   2 marks

3. Look at the coins below.

   a) How many coins are there in total? ....

   b) What is the total value of the coins? .... p

   2 marks

Challenge 2

1. Put the coins in order from **least** valuable to **most** valuable.

   least valuable [ ] [ ] [ ] [ ] [ ] [£2] most valuable

   6 marks

80

2. Put this money in order from **least** valuable to **most** valuable.

least valuable [ ][ ][ ][ ][ ] most valuable

3 marks

Challenge 3

1. Paulo has sorted his money into sets of the same coins. What is the value of each set of coins?

a)  .... P

b)  .... P

c)  .... P

d)  .... P

4 marks

How am I doing?   Total marks: [ ] /19

Measurement   81

Money problems

Challenge 1

1 Josh has bought some items for the beach!

a) Josh bought 3 kites. They were 2p each.

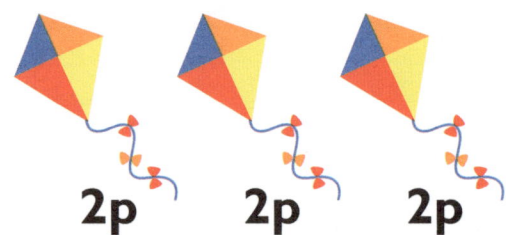

2p   2p   2p

How much did he spend? ....

b) The bucket and spade were 10p each.

How much did Josh spend

buying them both? ....

10p   10p

c) The ball and sunglasses were 5p each.

5p   5p

How much did Josh spend buying them both? ....

3 marks

Challenge 2

1 Solve these money problems.

Apple   **Banana**   **Lemon**   **Lime**

a) One apple costs 10p.

How much do 2 apples cost? .... p

b) Jess buys 2 bananas for 40p.

How much does each banana cost? .... p

c) Lemons are 10p each.

How much would 3 lemons be? .... p

d) Limes are £1 per bag. Eli has £2.

How many bags can he buy? ....

4 marks

Challenge 3

1. Mary has sorted her money into coins of the same type. Find the total of each set of Mary's coins.

   a) Mary has **four** 10p coins.

   The total amount is .... p.

   b) She has **eight** 2p coins.

   The total amount is .... p.

   c) Mary has **ten** 5p coins.

   The total amount is .... p.

   d) Mary has **two** 20p coins.

   The total amount is .... p.

   e) Mary has **two** 50p coins. Circle the amount she has in 50p coins.

   £1   £2   £4

5 marks

How am I doing?

Total marks: .... / 12

2-D shapes

Challenge 1

1. 2-D shapes are also known as **flat shapes**. Choosing from the given words, write the correct name next to each shape.

| hexagon | triangle | pentagon | circle | rectangle |

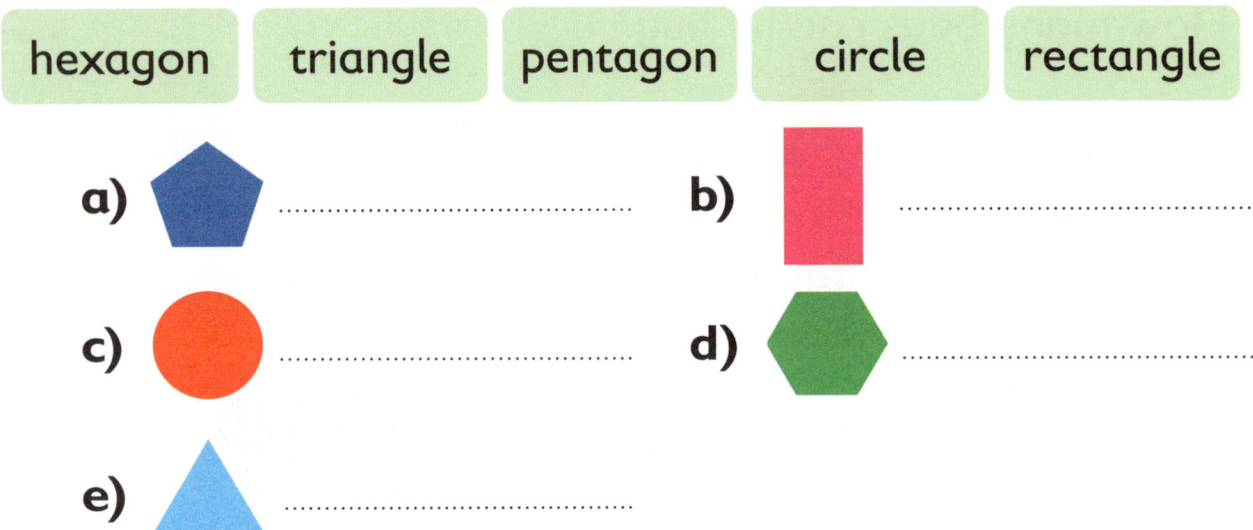

a) .... b) ....

c) .... d) ....

e) ....

5 marks

2. Count the number of each 2-D shape.

a) There are .... triangles.

b) There are .... squares.

c) There are .... hexagons.

d) There are .... circles.

e) How many shapes are there in total? ....

5 marks

84

Challenge 2

1. A triangle has three straight sides. Draw circles around the two identical triangles.

2 marks

Challenge 3

1. Name three items that are usually rectangular in shape. For example, a smartphone.

   a) ....

   b) ....

   c) ....

3 marks

2. Circle the shapes that are **not** rectangles.

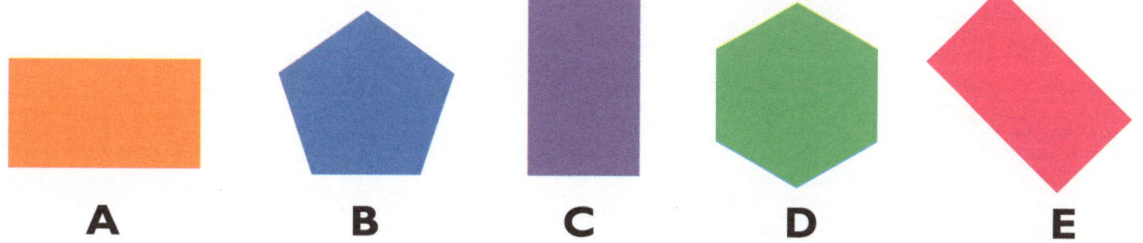

2 marks

How am I doing?   Total marks: ___ /17

Geometry – Properties of shapes   85

3-D shapes

Challenge 1

1) 3-D shapes are also known as **solid shapes**.

   Draw lines to match each 3-D shape to its name.

   cube   pyramid   cylinder   cuboid

   4 marks

2) Count the number of each 3-D shape.

   a) There are .... cubes.

   b) There are .... cylinders.

   c) There are .... cuboids.

   3 marks

Challenge 2

1. Circle the objects that are cylinders.

3 marks

Challenge 3

1. Name four items that are usually cuboid in shape. For example, a box of breakfast cereal.

   a) ....

   b) ....

   c) ....

   d) ....

4 marks

How am I doing?   Total marks: ☐ / 14

Geometry – Properties of shapes   87

Different shapes

Challenge 1

1. Draw and label five different 2-D shapes in the boxes below.

5 marks

Challenge 2

1. Name these shapes.

   a) ▨ This shape is a ....

   b) ◺ This shape is a ....

   c) ⬠ This shape is a ....

   d) ● This shape is a ....

4 marks

Challenge 3

1. Everyday objects can resemble 3-D (solid) shapes. Look around your home or school, and at pictures in books.

   Draw or write the name of different shaped objects in the table below.

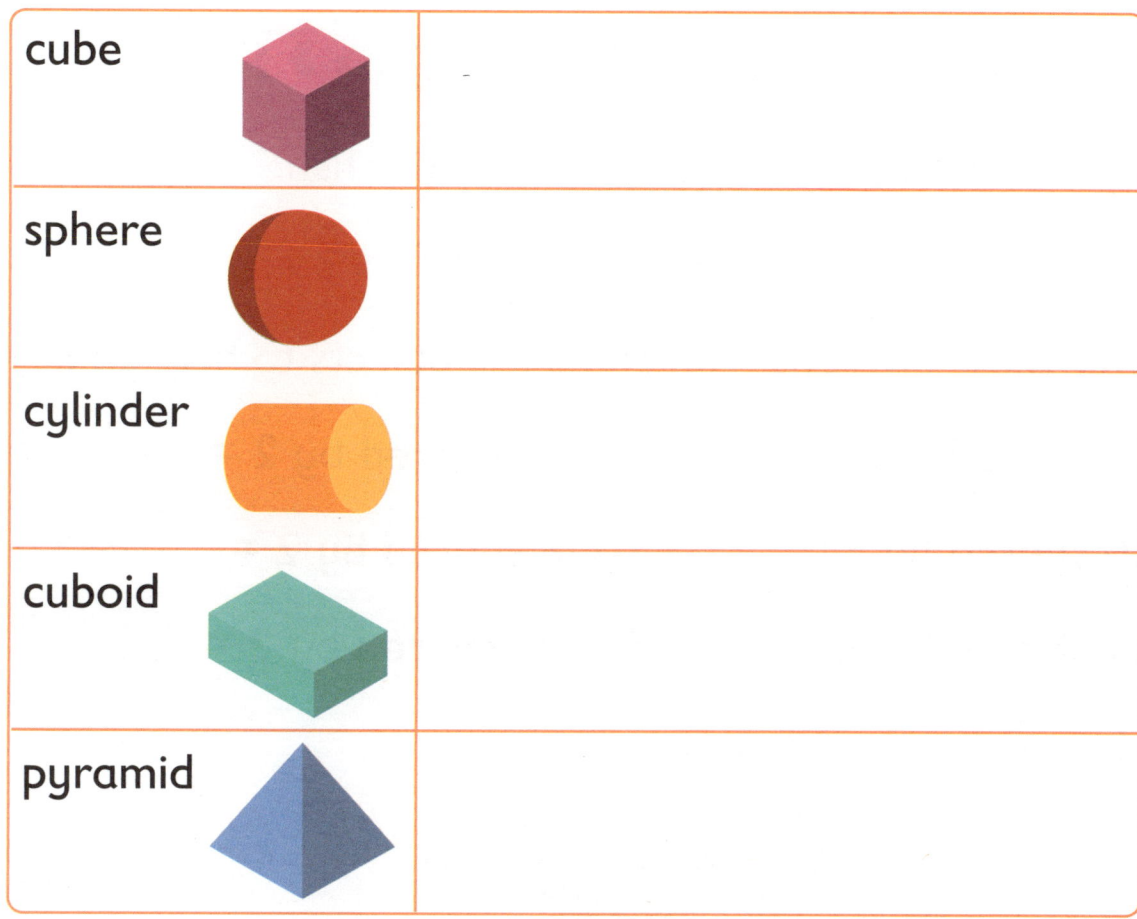

cube	
sphere	
cylinder	
cuboid	
pyramid	

5 marks

How am I doing?   Total marks: ☐ /14

Geometry – Properties of shapes

Progress test 3

1. Look at the fish. There are 12 in total.

   a) Draw a blue circle around half of the fish.

   b) Draw a red circle around $\frac{1}{4}$ of the fish.

   2 marks

2. Answer these divisions. You could use objects to help you.

   a) 6 shared by 2 = ...   b) 12 shared by 2 = ...

   c) 10 shared by 2 = ...   d) 8 shared by 2 = ...

   e) 14 shared by 2 = ...   f) 20 shared by 2 = ...

   6 marks

3. Bessie is collecting cherries.

   a) Each bowl holds 20 cherries. Bessie collects 2 bowlfuls. How many cherries has she collected? ....

   b) Bessie puts her cherries into groups of 10. How many groups of 10 does she have? ....

   c) Bessie shares all of her cherries with her brother Bobby. How many cherries do they get each? ....

   3 marks

4. Answer these capacity questions.

   a) If the capacity of one jug is 3 litres, what is the capacity of 2 jugs? .... litres

   b) Mila buys 5 litres of water.

   How many 1 litre bottles can she fill? ....

   c) Haroon needs to fill his 20 litre fish tank. He has a 2 litre container.

   How many containers will he use to fill the tank? ....

   d) Arlo has 100 ml of ice cream.

   How many 10 ml scoops can he serve? ....

5. Find $\frac{1}{2}$ of each of these groups of penguins.

   a)  $\frac{1}{2}$ = ...

   b)  $\frac{1}{2}$ = ...

6. Choose the correct words from the boxes to describe each pair of numbers.

   | is less than | is greater than | is equal to |

   a) 10 12

   b) 20 18

   c) 20 20

   d) 8 16

7. a) A worm measures exactly 20 cm.

    What does half of the worm measure? .... cm

    b) What would be the total length of 2 worms? .... cm

    c) How many worms would be needed to measure

    1 m (or 100 cm)? ....

8. Draw hands on the clocks to show the times.

    a) 2 o'clock   b) Half past 10   c) 8 o'clock

    d) Half past 7   e) 12 o'clock

9. Put the weights in order from lightest to heaviest.

    lightest   heaviest

10. Look at these numbers.

a) What is the highest value two-digit number you can make with these numbers? ....

b) What is the lowest value two-digit number you can make with these numbers? ....

2 marks

11. Divide the zebras into equal groups.

a)  = ... groups of 2

b)  = ... groups of 2

2 marks

12. Name these 3-D shapes.

a)  This 3-D shape is a ....

b)  This 3-D shape is a ....

c)  This 3-D shape is a ....

3 marks

How am I doing?   Total marks: .... / 39

Top, middle and bottom

Challenge 1

1 Here is a set of squares.

   a) Colour the **top** square red.

   b) Colour the **bottom** square blue.

   c) Colour the **middle** square green.

   3 marks

2 Here is a set of circles. Answer the questions using these words:

   | stripes | squares | spots |

   a) What pattern is in the **middle** circle?

   ....

   b) How is the **top** circle filled?

   ....

   c) What pattern does the **bottom** circle contain? ....

   3 marks

Challenge 2

1 Look at the shapes.

   a) Which shape is at the **bottom**?

   ....

   b) Which shape is in the **middle**?

   ....

   c) What is the name of the **top** shape?

   ....

   3 marks

Challenge 3

1 Look at the boxes.

    a) Draw a funny face in the **middle** box.

    b) Draw a star in the **top** box.

    c) Draw an apple in the **bottom** box.

3 marks

2 Now look at the squares on the right.

    a) Colour the **top** 2 squares yellow.

    b) Colour the **middle** 2 squares red.

    c) Colour the **bottom** 2 squares green.

3 marks

How am I doing?

Total marks: / 15

Geometry – Position and direction

Around, inside and outside

Challenge 1

1. **a)** Draw dots around the **outside** of this square.

   b) Draw four circles **inside** the square.

   2 marks

2. **a)** Draw four Xs around the **outside** of the circle.

   b) Draw dots **inside** the circle.

   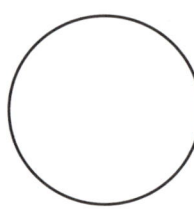

   2 marks

Challenge 2

1. Look at the shapes on the right.

   a) Which two shapes are on the **inside**?

   .... and

   ....

   b) Which shape is **outside** both of the other shapes?

   ....

   2 marks

2. Look at the shapes on the right.

   a) Which two shapes is the square **inside**?

   .... and

   ....

   b) Which shape is on the **outside**?

   ....

   2 marks

Challenge 3

1 Look at the square below.

a) Draw four circles around the **outside** of the square.

b) Draw a dot **inside** each circle.

c) Draw a triangle **inside** the square.

d) Draw an X **inside** the triangle.

4 marks

How am I doing?   Total marks: / 12

Geometry – Position and direction

Describing positions

Challenge 1

1. Buddy the cat is a little lost! He needs help to find his way home.

dog   **Buddy**   **sunflower**

a) If Buddy turns to your **right**, what will he see?

....

b) If he turns to your **left**, what will he see? ....

c) Draw a flower to the **right** of the sunflower.

d) Draw a ball **between** the dog and Buddy.

4 marks

Challenge 2

1. Help Agneta with her directions! She is facing the gnome.

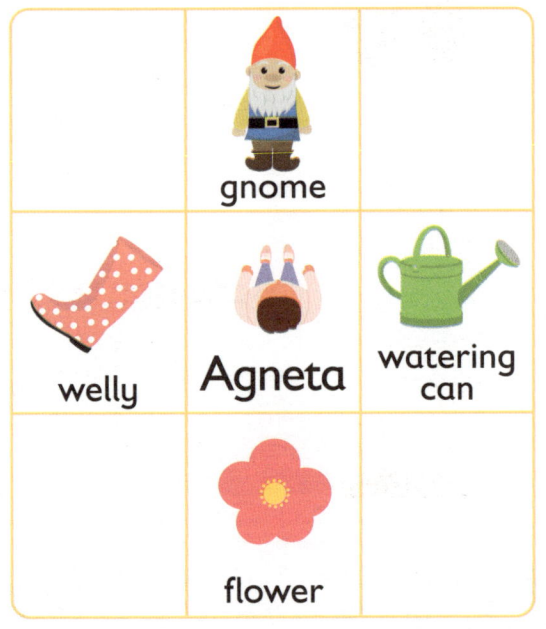

98

a) What is **in front of** Agneta? ....

b) What is **behind** Agneta? ....

c) What is to the **right** of Agneta? ....

d) What is to the **left** of Agneta? ....

4 marks

Challenge 3

1) Draw the items below in the correct places on the grid.

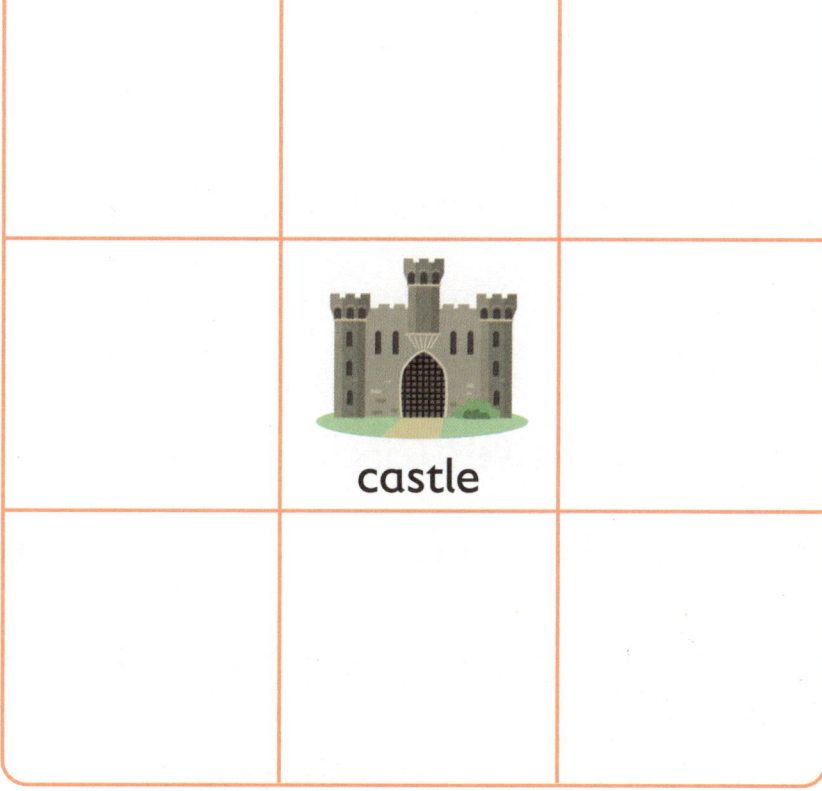

castle

a) Draw a star **above** the castle.

b) Draw a key **below** the castle.

c) Draw a coin to the **right** of the castle.

d) Draw a crown to the **left** of the castle.

4 marks

How am I doing?   Total marks: ▢ /12

Geometry – Position and direction   99

Left and right turns

Challenge 1

1. Look at the image below.

   a) Start at the cross and follow the arrows. Then make a **right** turn. What is there? ....

   b) What would be there if you made a **left** turn instead? ....

   2 marks

2. Is this sentence **true** or **false**? Circle your answer.

   Clockwise is a turn to the right.   True   False

   1 mark

Challenge 2

1. Look at the purple arrow on the right – it is pointing straight up.

   Choose from the white arrows **A**, **B** and **C** below to answer the questions.

   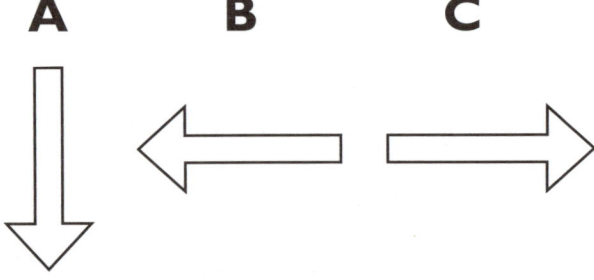

100

a) If the purple arrow turned a $\frac{1}{4}$ clockwise turn, which white arrow would it be?

b) If the purple arrow turned a half turn to the left or right, which white arrow would show its final position?

c) If the purple arrow turned a quarter turn to the left, which white arrow would it be?

3 marks

Challenge 3

1 Write down the directions to the house. Follow the path as shown by the arrows. The first one is done for you.

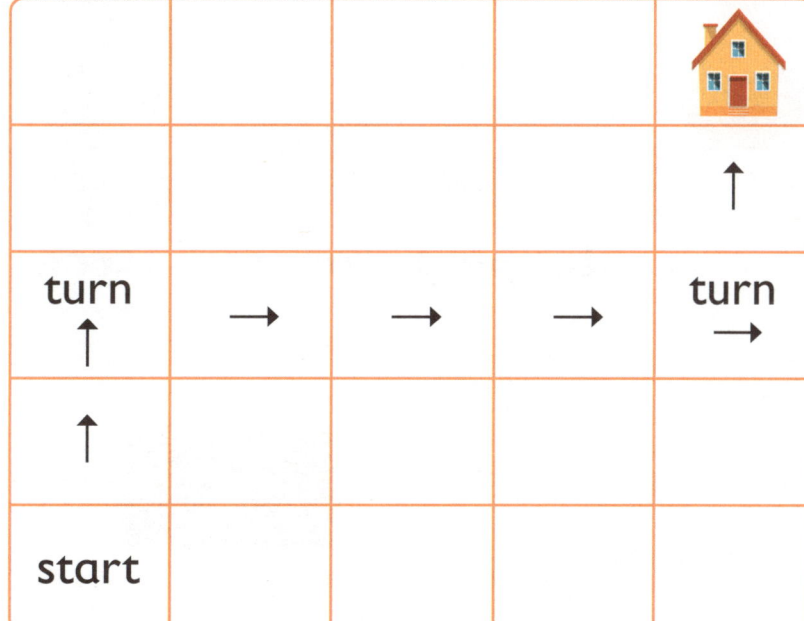

a) Move .... forwards 2 .... blocks.

b) Turn ....

c) Move .... blocks.

d) Turn ....

e) Move .... blocks.

4 marks

How am I doing?   Total marks: / 10

Geometry – Position and direction   101

More position and direction

Challenge 1

1. Help Charlie to make his journey.

   Choose the correct words from the boxes to pass each obstacle. The arrows help you choose the correct words.

   | through | around | across | under | over |

   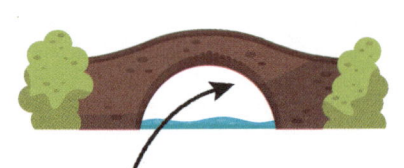
   bridge

   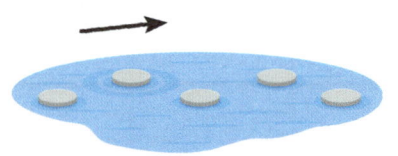
   stepping stones

   tree

   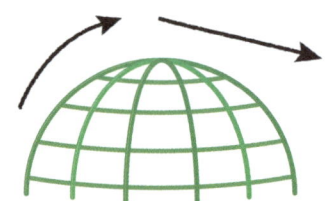
   climbing frame

   pipe

   a) Charlie should go .... the bridge.

   b) He should go .... the stepping stones.

   c) Charlie needs to go .... the tree.

   d) He should go .... the climbing frame.

   e) Charlie needs to go .... the pipe.

   5 marks

Challenge 2

1 Sana wanted a fun photo. Help her to describe it to her friends.

a) What is on top of Sana's head?

....

b) What is Sana standing on top of?

....

c) Sana is between the ....

and the ....

4 marks

Challenge 3

1 Use words from the boxes to describe Anya's challenge.

| up | down | under | across |

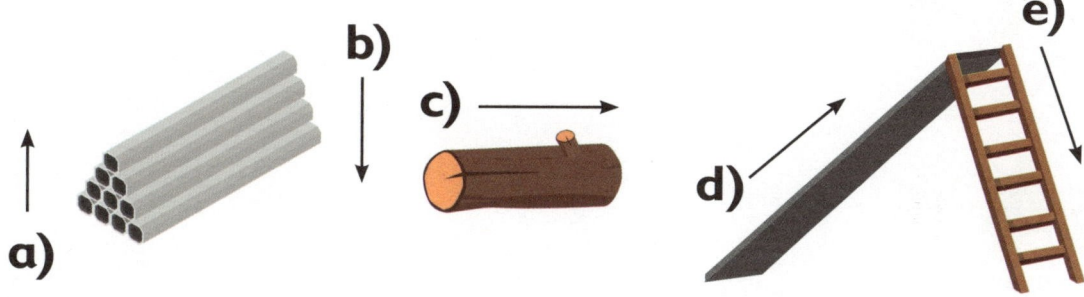

Anya climbed **a)** .... the obstacle, then

b) .... the other side, **c)** .... the

log, **d)** .... the ramp and **e)** ....

the ladder.

5 marks

How am I doing?   Total marks: ▢ /14

Geometry – Position and direction   103

Progress test 4

1. Write each set of numbers in order from **least** to **greatest**.

   a) 3 13 11 2   ☐ ☐ ☐ ☐

   b) 17 7 15 27   ☐ ☐ ☐ ☐

   c) 1 9 6 4   ☐ ☐ ☐ ☐

   6 marks

2. Write the addition and subtraction families for these sets of numbers. One is done for you.

   a) 3 2 5

   $3 + 2 = 5$ $2 + 3 = 5$ $5 - 3 = 2$ $5 - 2 = 3$

   b) 6 4 10

   ....

   c) 5 6 11

   ....

   2 marks

3. Flowers are sold in bunches of 5. There are 4 bunches of flowers. How many flowers are there altogether?

   ....

   1 mark

4. Use division to halve each number.

> **Example:** Half of 10 is 5

a) Half of 16 is ....

b) Half of 8 is ....

c) Half of 22 is ....

d) Half of 18 is ....

e) Half of 30 is ....

5 marks

5. Look at the skittle on the left.

Circle the skittle that would be a **quarter turn clockwise**.

 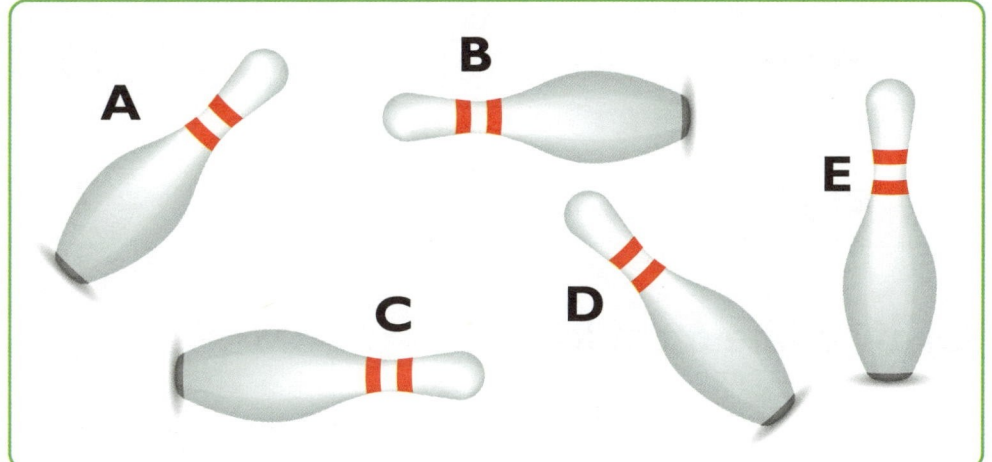

1 mark

6. Write the answers to these additions.

a) 2 + 2 + 2 = ...

b) 10 + 10 + 10 = ...

c) 5 + 5 + 5 + 5 = ...

3 marks

Progress test 4

7. Jenny has 6 rings. She loses 2 rings.

How many rings does she now have? ....

8. Hameed sets off to school at **8** o'clock in the morning. He arrives at **9** o'clock morning time.

How many hours did the journey take? Circle the correct answer.

| **1 hour** | **2 hours** | **3 hours** |

2 marks

9. Draw lines to match the words to the numerals.

sixteen	9
seven	8
nine	16
eight	7

4 marks

10. a) Draw a line 6 cm long.

b) Draw a line 3 cm long.

2 marks

11. Look at the grid below.

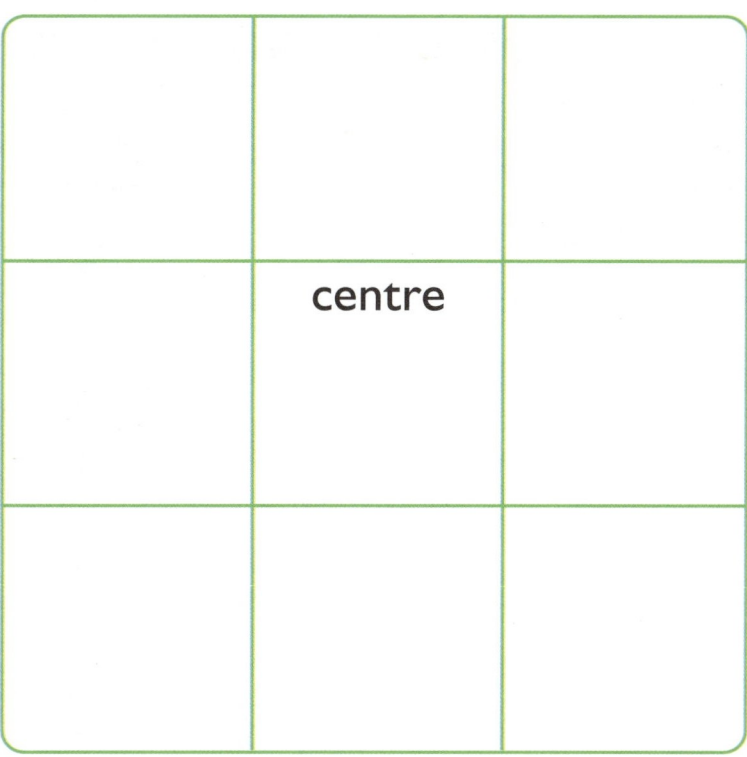

Add the following to the grid.

a) Draw a triangle in the centre.

b) Draw a tick (✓) **above** the triangle.

c) Draw a square **below** the triangle.

d) Draw a circle to the **right** of the triangle.

e) Draw a cross (✗) to the **left** of the triangle.

5 marks

12. Shade or colour in the fractions of each circle.

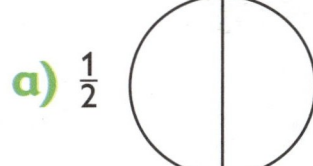 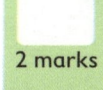

2 marks

Answers

For questions worth one mark with several answer spaces, all answers should be correct to achieve the mark, unless otherwise indicated.

Pages 4–11 Starter test

1. a) 1, **2**, 3, 4, **5**, 6, **7**, 8, **9**, 10
   b) 2, **4**, 6, **8**, 10, **12**, 14, **16**, **18**, 20
   c) 0, 5, 10, 15, **20**, 25, 30
2. a) 3, 4, **5**
   b) 8, 9, **10**
   c) 5, 6, **7**
   d) 7, 8, **9**
   e) 4, 5, **6**
   f) **6**, **7**, **8**
3. **A** and **C** ticked
4. a) 12 counters drawn
   b) 17 counters drawn
5. a) true
   b) false
   c) true
6. a) 7   b) 15   c) 4   d) 20
   e) 17   f) 0
7. a) 6 eggs
   b) 2 + 2 + 2 = 6 (**or** 3 lots of 2 = 6)
8. a) twelve   b) ten
   c) seven   d) six
   e) zero   f) fourteen
   g) eleven   h) five
   i) nine   j) sixteen
9. a) 10 apples
   b) 5 + 5 = 10 (**or** 2 lots of 5 = 10)
   c) 15 apples
   d) 5 + 5 + 5 = 15 (**or** 3 lots of 5 = 15)
10. a) 3 + 1 = 5 circled
    b) 2 + 2 = 6 circled
    c) 14 − 5 = 10 circled
11. a) 3 o'clock
    b) 9 o'clock
    c) 5 o'clock
12. a) C   b) shorter   c) D
    d) C, A, B, D (1 mark for 2 snakes in correct order; 2 marks for all correct)
13. 1
14. a) 16   b) 20   c) 30   d) 24
15. a) 6   b) 8   c) 10   d) 12
16. a) 6   b) 4   c) 9
17. a) **B** and **C** ticked
    b) Sequence **A** is counting backwards / down in 1s
       Sequence **B** is counting forwards / up in 1s
    c) **C** ticked
       An indication that it is counting backwards while the others are counting forwards
18. a) 1 ten, 5 ones
    b) 1 ten, 6 ones drawn
    c) 2 tens, 9 ones drawn
19. a) 7   b) 8
20. a) 17   b) 15
21. heaviest

    lightest

Pages 12–13

Challenge 1

1. a) 11 circled

b) 2, 3, 6, 11 (1 mark for 2 or 3 numbers in correct order; 2 marks for all correct)

2. a) 32 ticked
   b) 14, 18, 22, 24, 32 (1 mark for 2 numbers in correct order; 2 marks for 3 or 4 correct; 3 marks for all correct)

Challenge 2
1. a) 2 tens, 6 ones
   b) 20 + 6
2. a) 10, or 1 ten
   b) 3 or 3 ones
   c) 20 or 2 tens

Challenge 3
1.

1	2	3	4	5	6	7	8	9	10
11	12	**13**	**14**	15	**16**	**17**	**18**	**19**	20
21	**22**	23	24	**25**	**26**	**27**	**28**	29	**30**
31	**32**	33	**34**	**35**	36	**37**	**38**	**39**	**40**
41	**42**	**43**	**44**	**45**	**46**	**47**	48	**49**	**50**
51	**52**	**53**	**54**	55	**56**	**57**	**58**	59	**60**
61	**62**	63	**64**	**65**	**66**	67	**68**	**69**	**70**
71	**72**	**73**	**74**	**75**	**76**	77	78	**79**	**80**
81	**82**	**83**	84	**85**	**86**	**87**	**88**	**89**	90
91	**92**	**93**	**94**	**95**	**96**	97	**98**	99	**100**

(1 mark for each correct row)

Pages 14–15
Challenge 1
1. a) 14 b) 9 c) 7 d) 5
2. a) 7 b) 10 c) 12 d) 15

Challenge 2
1. 7
2. 17
3. 10, **9**, 8, **7**, 6, **5**, 4, 3, 2, **1**

Challenge 3
1. 20, 19, 15, 14, 13, 5, 4 (1 mark for 2 numbers in correct order; 2 marks for 3 correct; 3 marks for 4 correct; 4 marks for 5 or 6 correct; 5 marks for all correct)
2. a)

1	2	3
11	12	**13**
21	**22**	**23**

b)

23	24	25
33	34	35
43	44	45

Pages 16–17
Challenge 1
1. a) 2, 4, 6, 8, **10**, **12**, **14**, **16**
   b) 15, 13, 11, **9**, **7**, **5**, **3**
2. a) 2
   b) 5

Challenge 2
1. a) 15, **20**, **25**, 30, 35, **40**
   b) 20, **25**, **30**, 35, **40**, **45**
2. a) backwards
   b) forwards

Challenge 3
1. a) **5**, 10, **15**, 20
   b) 2, **4**, **6**, **8**
2. true

Pages 18–19
Challenge 1
1. 30
2. 2
3.

| 10 | **20** | 30 | 40 | **50** | 60 | 70 | **80** |

(1 mark for 3–5 numbers correct; 2 marks for all correct)

4. 40

Challenge 2
1. 10, 20, 30, 40, 50 (1 mark for 2 numbers in correct order; 2 marks for 3 or 4 correct; 3 marks for all correct)
2. 40, 50, 60, 70, 80 (1 mark for 2 numbers in correct order; 2 marks for 3 or 4 correct; 3 marks for all correct)

Challenge 3
1. a) 3 b) 6 c) 5 d) 4

Pages 20–21
Challenge 1
1. a) **14**, 15, **16**
   b) **17**, 18, **19**
   c) 8, 9, **10**
   d) 18, 19, **20**
   e) **16**, 17, **18**
2. a) 4 b) 6 c) 13

Answers

Challenge 2
1. a) 7 b) 17 c) 25 d) 15
2. a) 16 b) 29 c) 11 d) 24
3. 19

Challenge 3
1. a) 4 b) 16 c) 30 d) 22
2. a) 10 b) 10
3. a) 30
   b) 50
      20 + 30 = 50 **or** 20 + 20 + 10 = 50

Pages 22–23
Challenge 1
1. a) 21 b) 15 c) 29 d) 43
2. a) 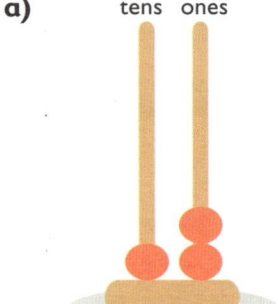 b)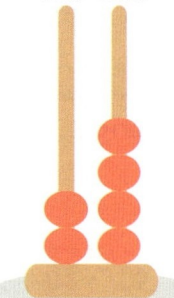
   c) 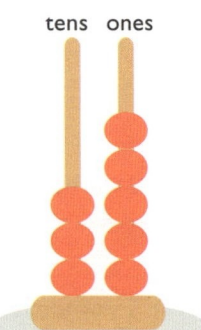 d)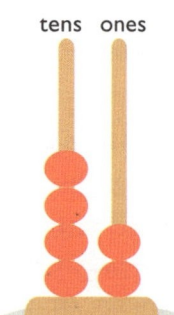

Challenge 2
1. a) 10 + 2
   b) 20 + 5
   c) 30 + 8
   d) 40 + 6
2. a) 25 b) 31 c) 42 d) 37

Challenge 3
1. 2, 15, 16, 28 (1 mark for 2 or 3 numbers in correct order; 2 marks for all correct)
2. a) 1 ten, 4 ones
   b) 2 tens, 4 ones
   c) 3 tens, 6 ones
   d) 4 tens, 8 ones
3. Accept 12, 13 or 14
4. Accept 16, 17, 18 or 19

Challenge 1
1. a) Any pair where the first number is less than the second, e.g. 17 and 20
   b) Any pair where the first number is greater than the second, e.g. 26 and 14
   c) 1 and 1 **or** 20 and 20
2. a) Any pair where the first number is greater than the second
   b) Any pair where the first number is less than the second
   c) Any pair of equal numbers

Challenge 2
1. a) is less than b) is equal to
   c) is greater than
2. a) is less than b) is greater than
   c) is equal to

Challenge 3
1. a) equal b) fewer
   c) fewer d) more

Pages 26–27
Challenge 1
1. a) 4 counters drawn
   b) 8 counters drawn
   c) 10 counters drawn
2. a) 4 b) 6 c) 8 d) 10

Challenge 2
1. a) 2 counters crossed out
   b) 5 counters crossed out
   c) 4 counters crossed out
   d) 6 counters crossed out
2. a) 4 b) 5 c) 2 d) 3

Challenge 3
1. a) Double 5 is 10, half of 10 = 5
   b) Double 7 is 14, half of 14 = 7
2. a) 2 + 2 = 4 b) 6 + 6 = 12
   c) 10 + 10 = 20 d) 8 + 8 = 16

Pages 28–29

Challenge 1
1. a) 7 + 5 = 12
   b) 10 + 7 = 17
   c) 5 + 5 = 10

Challenge 2
1. a) 12 – 3 = 9
   b) 10 – 4 = 6

Challenge 3
1. a) 3 + 1 + 5 = 9 or 3 + 5 + 1 = 9 or 1 + 5 + 3 = 9 or 1 + 3 + 5 = 9 or 5 + 1 + 3 = 9
   b) 4 + 3 + 2 = 9 or 4 + 2 + 3 = 9 or 2 + 3 + 4 = 9 or 2 + 4 + 3 = 9 or 3 + 2 + 4 = 9
   c) 1 + 5 + 6 = 12 or 1 + 6 + 5 = 12 or 5 + 1 + 6 = 12 or 5 + 6 + 1 = 12 or 6 + 5 + 1 = 12

Pages 30–31

Challenge 1
1. 1 + 9, 9 + 1, 8 + 2, 2 + 8, 3 + 7, 7 + 3, 4 + 6, 6 + 4, 5 + 5, 0 + 10, 10 + 0

Challenge 2
1. a)–j) Any two-digit numbers using two different one-digit numbers available.
2. a) 13 b) 14 c) 16 d) 11
   e) 18

Challenge 3
1. Any five subtractions that correctly result in 10 as the answer.
2. 20, 19, **18**, 17, **16**, 15, **14**

Pages 32–33

Challenge 1
1. a) 6 b) 2 c) 4 d) 3
   e) 7 f) 10 g) 7 h) 2

Challenge 2
1. a) 4 b) 4 c) 2 d) 1
   e) 12 f) 12 g) 17 h) 10
2. a) + b) + c) –
   d) + e) –

Challenge 3
1. a) 8p b) 15p
   c) 17p (Accept 2p more than answer to part b))
   d) 23p (Accept sum of answers to parts a) and b))
   e) 4p

Pages 34–35

Challenge 1
1. a) false b) true c) false
2. a) 19 b) 21 c) 15

Challenge 2
1. a) 15 b) 15, 16, 17, 18, 19, 20
   c) 22 d) 5

Challenge 3
1. a) ✓ b) ✓ c) ✗
2. a) 7 b) 12 – 5 = 7
3. a) true b) false
4. a) 20
   b) Accept any four subtractions that leave 5

Progress test 1

Pages 36–39

1. a) 10
   b) 8
   c) 20
   d) 12
2. a) 1 b) 2 c) 5 d) 10
3. Any eight two-digit numbers using the digits 1, 2, 3, 4, 5
4. a) 7
   b) 4 (Accept 3 less than answer to part a))
   c) 10 (Accept 6 more than answer to part b))
5. a) 3 + 9 = 12
   b) 8 + 2 = 10
   c) 4 + 7 = 11
6. 20 circled
7. a) 7 b) 14 c) 16 d) 20
8. a) 21 b) 15 c) 11
9. a) 4 b) 5 c) 15 d) 11
10. a) five
    b) seven
    c) nine
    d) two
    e) twelve
11.

1	5	4
1	3	6
8	2	0

12. a) 12 b) 98
    c) Any odd number possible from the given numbers.
    d) Any even number possible from the given numbers.

Answers 111

13. a) 14 + 5 = 19, 5 + 14 = 19, 19 – 14 = 5,
       19 – 5 = 14
    b) 11 + 4 = 15, 4 + 11 = 15, 15 – 11 = 4,
       15 – 4 = 11
14. Stars put into three groups of 5
15. 13

Pages 40–41

Challenge 1
1. a) 10
   b) 5 sets of 2 = 10
2. a) 3 sets of 2 = 6
   b) 2 sets of 5 = 10
   c) 3 sets of 10 = 30

Challenge 2
1. 5 sets of 2 = 10, 2 sets of 5 = 10
2. (1 mark for correct number of rows, 1 mark for correct number of columns)
   a)
   b) 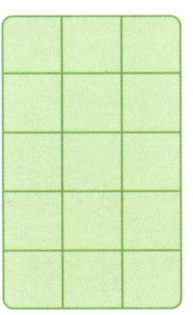   c)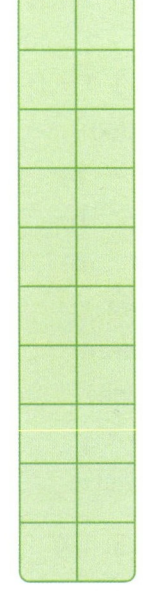

Challenge 3
1.
Addition	Number of sets
2 + 2 + 2 + 2 + 2 = 10	5 sets of 2
5 + 5 + 5 = 15	3 sets of 5
10 + 10 + 10 = 30	**3 sets of 10**
5 + 5 + 5 + 5 = 20	4 sets of 5
10 + 10 + 10 + 10 + 10 = 50	5 sets of 10
2 + 2 + 2 + 2 + 2 + 2 = 12	**6 sets of 2**

Pages 42–43

Challenge 1
1. a) 2   b) 3   c) 5

Challenge 2
1. 4
2. 6
3. 3

Challenge 3
1.
Number of items	Number of people	They each get
6	2	3
14	2	7
16	2	8
18	2	9
20	2	10

Pages 44–45

Challenge 1
1. Correct number of counters and correct totals indicated in each box

Challenge 2
1.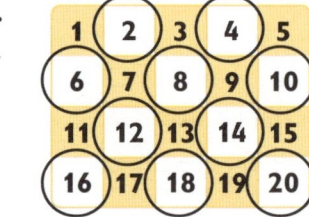

(1 mark for each correct row)

2. a) false
   b) true

112

Challenge 3
1. a) 2 times 4 = 8
   b) 10 times 1 = 10
2. a) 3 times 2 = 6, 2 times 3 = 6
   b) 5 times 2 = 10, 2 times 5 = 10

Pages 46–47
Challenge 1
1. 6 shared by 2 = 3
2. a) 10 shared by 2 = 5 **or** 10 shared by 5 = 2
   b) 20 shared by 10 = 2 **or** 20 shared by 2 = 10
   c) 16 shared by 2 = 8 **or** 16 shared by 8 = 2
3. a) 18 shared by 2 = 9 **or** 18 shared by 9 = 2
   b) 8 shared by 2 = 4 **or** 8 shared by 4 = 2
   c) 12 shared by 6 = 2 **or** 12 shared by 2 = 6

Challenge 2
1. a) 10
   b) 20 shared by 2 = 10
   c) 5

Challenge 3
1. a) 2   b) 4   c) 10

Pages 48–49
Challenge 1
1. a) 10   b) 20   c) 6
2. a) 2   b) 4   c) 5

Challenge 2
1. a) 10   b) 5
2. a) 10   b) 20, Drawing of 20 flowers

Challenge 3
1. a) 10   b) 2   c) 4   d) 1

Pages 50–51
Challenge 1
1. a) 5   b) 10
2. a) 8   b) 4

Challenge 2
1. a) 10   b) 5   c) 2
2. a) 10   b) 3

Challenge 3
1. a) 4 spots
   b) 20 boys
   c) 30 stickers

Pages 52–53
Challenge 1
1. a) 3   b) 6   c) 10   d) even   e) odd

Challenge 2
1. a) 4   b) 5   c) 7

Challenge 3
1. a) 15
       20 − 5 = 15
   b) 5
   c) 10

Pages 54–55
Challenge 1
1. a) 2   b) 3   c) 6

Challenge 2
1. 6
2. a) 4   b) 5   c) 6
3. a) false
   b) true

Challenge 3
1. a) 8
   b) 4 groups of 2 = 8
2. a) 10
   b) 2 groups of 5 = 10
3. a) ✓   b) ✗   c) ✗   d) ✓

Pages 56–57
Challenge 1
1. a) ✓   b) ✗
   c) ✗   d) ✓
   e) ✗   f) ✓

Challenge 2
1. a)–d) Any one half of each circle shaded
2. 4

Challenge 3
1. a)–d) Any one half of each square shaded
2. 8

Pages 58–59
Challenge 1
1. **A** and **C** ticked
2. a)–d) Any one quarter of each shape shaded
3. a)–d) Any one quarter of each shape shaded

Challenge 2
1. a) ✗   b) ✗   c) ✗
   d) ✓   e) ✓

Challenge 3
1. a) 1 quarter
   b) 3 quarters
   c) 2 quarters
   d) 4 quarters

Answers

  e) 0 quarters
2. a) 3 quarters
   b) 1 quarter
   c) 2 quarters
   d) 0 quarters
   e) 4 quarters

Pages 60–61

Challenge 1
1. a) 3   b) 4   c) 5
   d) 6   e) 2

Challenge 2
1. a) 4   b) 8   c) 4

Challenge 3
1.

Items	Amount in $\frac{1}{4}$	Amount in $\frac{1}{2}$
4 stickers	1	2
20 buns	5	10
8 straws	2	4
12 apples	3	6

Pages 62–63

Challenge 1
1. a) 1   b) 3   c) 1   d) 2
2. $\frac{1}{2}$ – greater
   $\frac{1}{4}$ – smaller

Challenge 2
1. a) 6   b) 3   c) 8
   d) 5   e) 5
2. a) false   b) true   c) true
   d) false   e) true

Challenge 3
1. a) 8   b) 20   c) 20   d) 6   e) 16

Pages 64–65

Challenge 1
1. a) 6   b) 3   c) 1p

Challenge 2
1. a) 8   b) 4   c) 4   d) 2

Challenge 3
1. a) 6   b) 3
   c) 2   d) 4

Progress test 2

Pages 66–69
1. a) 9   b) 15   c) 11   d) 11
2. a) 2 tens, 7 ones
   b) 1 ten, 9 ones
   c) 2 tens, 1 one
   d) 2 tens, 5 ones
   e) 1 ten, 5 ones
3. a) 10   b) 5   c) 20
4. a) 8   b) 10   c) 4   d) 5   e) 7
5. a) 4   b) 10   c) 20   d) 16   e) 14
6. a)
   b)
7. a) 4   b) 10   c) 20
8. 0, 5, **10**, **15**, **20**, **25**
9. a) **12**, 13, **14**
   b) **10**, 11, **12**
   c) **18**, 19, **20**
10. a) is greater than
    b) is less than
    c) is greater than
    d) is equal to
    e) is less than
11. a) 3 + 5 = 8, 5 + 3 = 8
    b) 3 + 2 + 1 = 6 and 3, 2 and 1 added in any different order = 6
12. a) 1   b) 2   c) 6   d) 2

Pages 70–71

Challenge 1
1. B, D, E, C, A

Challenge 2
1. chair ⟶ about 1 m
   glue stick ⟶ less than 1 m
   milk ⟶ less than 1 m
   tree ⟶ about 3 m
   building ⟶ over 5 m
2. a) 3 cm   b) 9 cm

Challenge 3

1. a) D
   b) A
   c) shorter
   d) A, C, B, D (1 mark for 2 or 3 caterpillars in correct order; 2 marks for all correct)
   e) 15 cm
2. a) 3 m b) 2 m c) 1 m d) 2 m

Pages 72–73
Challenge 1

1. a) **A** circled
   b) **C** circled
   c) A, B, D, C (1 mark for 2 or 3 items in correct order; 2 marks for all correct)

Challenge 2

1. a) C, B, A
   b) **B** circled
   c) 6 litres ticked

Challenge 3

1. a) Ruby
   b) Fred
   c) Ali and Susie
   d) Ruby
   e) 3 kg (Ruby), 2 kg (Susie) and 2 kg (Ali) in either order, 1 kg (Fred) (1 mark for 2 weights in correct order; 2 marks for all correct)

Pages 74–75
Challenge 1

1. a) shorter
   b) Bella
   c) smallest / shortest
   d) Lukas

Challenge 2

1. a) 10
   b) 20 litres
   c) 30 litres
   d) 3

Challenge 3

1. a) B   b) 5 kg
   c) 3 kg   d) B and C

Pages 76–77
Challenge 1

1. a) Wednesday
   b) Tuesday
   c) Wednesday
2. January, February, March, April, May, June, July, August, September, October, November, December (1 mark for 4–7 months in correct order; 2 marks for 8–11 correct; 3 marks for all correct)

Challenge 2

1. a) 2 o'clock
   b) half past 4
   c) 3 o'clock
   d) half past 8
   e) 5 o'clock

Challenge 3

1.

Pages 78–79
Challenge 1

1. C, E, D, A, B (1 mark for 2 events in correct order; 2 marks for 3 or 4 correct; 3 marks for all correct)
2. a) before
   b) after
   c) first
   d) next

Challenge 2

1. a) tomorrow
   b) morning
   c) evening

Answers

2. a) decade circled
    b) days circled

Challenge 3
1. a) 1 o'clock drawn on clock B
    b) 12 o'clock
    c) 4 hours

Pages 80–81
Challenge 1
1. a) 7   b) 7p
2. a) 5   b) 10p
3. a) 4   b) 20p

Challenge 2
1. 1p, 2p, 5p, 10p, 20p, 50p, £1, £2 (1 mark for 2 coins in correct order; 2 marks for 3 correct; 3 marks for 4 correct; 4 marks for 5 correct; 5 marks for 6 or 7 correct; 6 marks for all correct)
2. 20p, £2, £5, £10, £20 (1 mark for 2 amounts in correct order; 2 marks for 3 or 4 correct; 3 marks for all correct)

Challenge 3
1. a) 16p   b) 35p
    c) 20p   d) 10p

Pages 82–83
Challenge 1
1. a) 6p   b) 20p   c) 10p

Challenge 2
1. a) 20p   b) 20p
    c) 30p   d) 2

Challenge 3
1. a) 40p   b) 16p   c) 50p
    d) 40p   e) £1 circled

Pages 84–85
Challenge 1
1. a) pentagon
    b) rectangle
    c) circle
    d) hexagon
    e) triangle
2. a) 4 b) 3 c) 3 d) 3 e) 13

Challenge 2
1. 2nd and 4th triangles circled

Challenge 3
1. a)–c) Accept any three items that are rectangles
2. **B** and **D** circled

Pages 86–87
Challenge 1
1.  – cylinder

     – cuboid

     – pyramid

    – cube

2. a) 2
    b) 2
    c) 4 (Accept 6 if including cubes as a special type of cuboid)

Challenge 2
1. Straw, food tin and glue stick circled

Challenge 3
1. a)–d) Accept any four items that are cuboids

Pages 88–89
Challenge 1
1. Accept drawings of any five different 2-D shapes that are identifiable from key features

Challenge 2
1. a) square
    b) triangle
    c) pentagon
    d) circle

Challenge 3
1. At least one appropriately shaped object to be drawn or named for each shape

Progress test 3

Pages 90–93

1. a) 6 fish circled in blue
   b) 3 fish circled in red
2. a) 3 b) 6 c) 5
   d) 4 e) 7 f) 10
3. a) 40 b) 4 c) 20
4. a) 6 litres
   b) 5
   c) 10
   d) 10
5. a) 3 b) 4
6. a) is less than
   b) is greater than
   c) is equal to
   d) is less than
7. a) 10 cm b) 40 cm c) 5
8. a)    b)
   c)    d)
   e)
9. 1 kg, 2 kg, 10 kg, 11 kg (1 mark for 2 weights in correct order; 2 marks for 3 weights in correct order; 3 marks for all correct)
10. a) 97 b) 36
11. a) 2 b) 3
12. a) cylinder
    b) cuboid
    c) sphere

Pages 94–95

Challenge 1
1. a) Top square coloured red
   b) Bottom square coloured blue
   c) Middle square coloured green
2. a) squares
   b) stripes
   c) spots

Challenge 2
1. a) triangle
   b) square
   c) circle

Challenge 3
1. a) A funny face drawn in the middle box
   b) A star drawn in the top box
   c) An apple drawn in the bottom box
2. a) Top two squares coloured yellow
   b) Middle two squares coloured red
   c) Bottom two squares coloured green

Pages 96–97

Challenge 1
1. a) Dots drawn around the outside of the square
   b) Four circles drawn inside the square
2. a) Four Xs drawn around the outside of the circle
   b) Dots drawn inside the circle

Challenge 2
1. a) triangle and circle
   b) square
2. a) circle and triangle
   b) triangle

Challenge 3
1. a) Four circles drawn around the outside of the square
   b) A dot drawn inside each of the four circles
   c) A triangle drawn inside the square
   d) An X drawn inside the triangle

Pages 98–99

Challenge 1
1. a) sunflower
   b) dog
   c) A flower drawn to the right of the sunflower.
   d) A ball drawn between the dog and Buddy.

Challenge 2
1. a) gnome
   b) flower
   c) (watering) can
   d) welly

Answers 117

Answers

Challenge 3

1.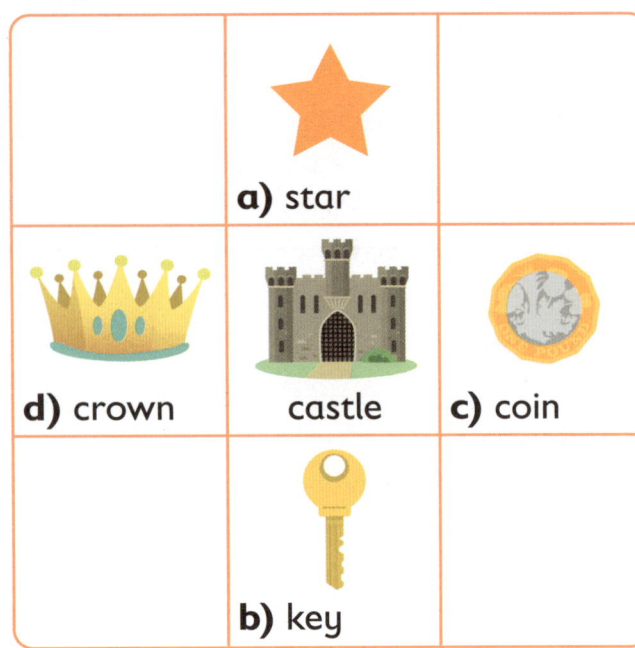

Pages 100–101

Challenge 1

1. a) ladybird   b) snail
2. True circled

Challenge 2

1. a) C   b) A   c) B

Challenge 3

1. b) $\frac{1}{4}$ turn right **or** $\frac{1}{4}$ turn clockwise
   c) forwards (right) 4
   d) $\frac{1}{4}$ turn left
   e) forwards (up) 2

Pages 102–103

Challenge 1

1. a) under
   b) across / over
   c) around
   d) over / across
   e) through

Challenge 2

1. a) bird / parrot
   b) box
   c) bird / parrot and box

Challenge 3

1. a) up   b) down   c) across
   d) up   e) down

Progress test 4

Pages 104–107

1. a) 2, 3, 11, 13 (1 mark for 2 or 3 numbers in correct order; 2 marks for all correct)
   b) 7, 15, 17, 27 (1 mark for 2 or 3 numbers in correct order; 2 marks for all correct)
   c) 1, 4, 6, 9 (1 mark for 2 or 3 numbers in correct order; 2 marks for all correct)
2. b) 6 + 4 = 10, 4 + 6 = 10, 10 − 6 = 4, 10 − 4 = 6
   c) 5 + 6 = 11, 6 + 5 = 11, 11 − 5 = 6, 11 − 6 = 5
3. 20
4. a) 8   b) 4   c) 11   d) 9   e) 15
5. **C** circled
6. a) 6   b) 30   c) 20
7. 4
8. 1 hour circled
9. sixteen – 16   seven – 7
   nine – 9   eight – 8
10. a) Accept any line measuring between 5 cm and 7 cm
    b) Accept any line measuring between 2 cm and 4 cm
11.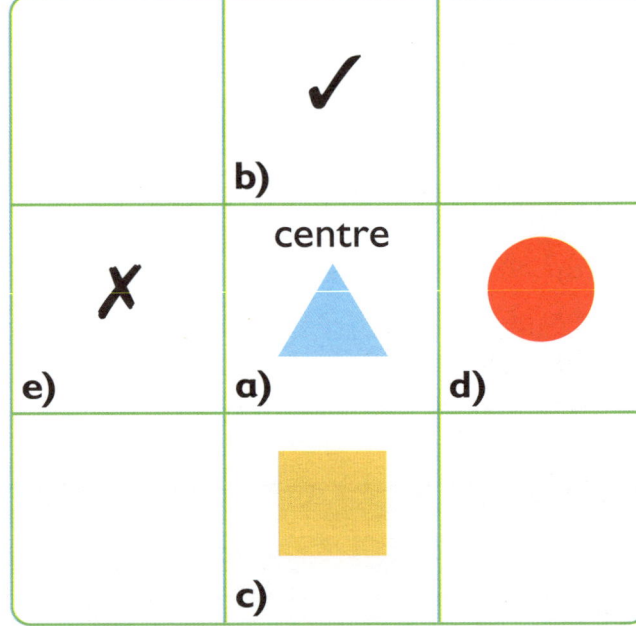
12. a) Any half of the circle coloured
    b) Any quarter of the circle coloured

118

Notes

Progress test charts

Use these charts to record your results in the four Progress Tests. Colour in the questions that you got right to help you identify any areas that you might need to study and practise again.
(These areas are indicated in the 'See page…' row in the charts.)

Progress test 1:

	Q1	Q2	Q3	Q4	Q5	Q6	Q7	Q8	Q9	Q10	Q11	Q12	Q13	Q14	Q15	TOTAL /50
See page…	26-27	26-27	30-31	28-29	28-29	20-21	12-13	22-23	16-19	12-13	14-15	12-13	32-33	18-19	28-29	

Progress test 2:

	Q1	Q2	Q3	Q4	Q5	Q6	Q7	Q8	Q9	Q10	Q11	Q12	TOTAL /47
See page…	28-29	12-13	60-61	48-49	48-49	40-41	50-51	44-45	20-21	24-25	28-29	60-61	

Progress test 3:

	Q1	Q2	Q3	Q4	Q5	Q6	Q7	Q8	Q9	Q10	Q11	Q12	TOTAL /39
See page…	60-61	46-47	28-29	72-73	60-61	24-25	70-71	76-77	72-73	22-23	42-43	86-87	

Progress test 4:

	Q1	Q2	Q3	Q4	Q5	Q6	Q7	Q8	Q9	Q10	Q11	Q12	TOTAL /33
See page…	12-13	28-29	40-41	42-43	100-101	20-21	28-29	78-79	12-13	70-71	98-99	56-57	

What am I doing well in? ....

....

What do I need to improve? ....

....